I Remember

When . . .

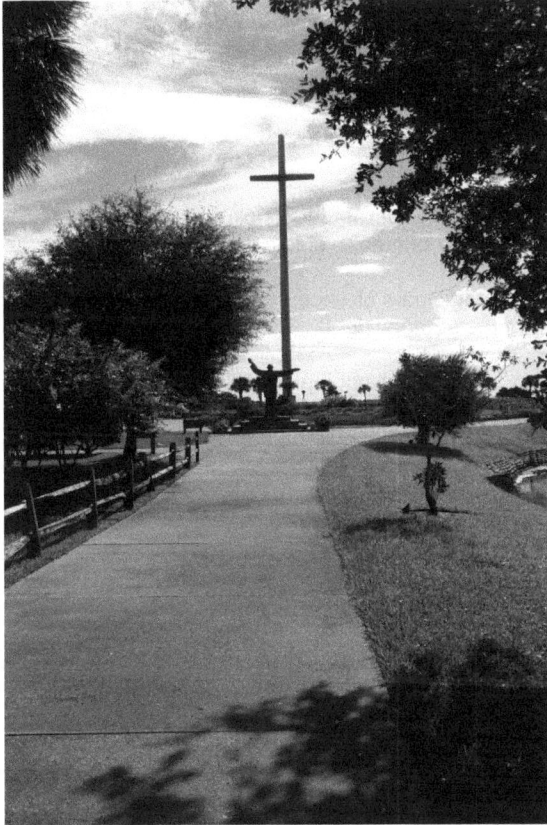

A small spiritual biography
By Brother Al

Greenbush Press
Spring, TX
SAN: 256-5048

I Remember When . . .

Book design, including all photographs by Alexander W. Salay

Requests for information should be addressed to:
Greenbush Press, 21518 Karpathos Ln., Spring, TX 77388-3262

Published simultaneously worldwide.

Alexander W. Salay (Brother Al)
BroAl@BlessedMan.net

ISBN 978-0-9766720-5-0
Library of Congress Control Number: 2014955921

Printed in the United States of America

I Remember When . . .

The presence
> *of God,*

The wooing
> *of His Holy Spirit,*

The glow
> *of His love,*

Made this life
> *BLESSED.*

CONTENTS

Introduction *1*

A Real Song *3*

Call Of The Radio...*7*

Lunch Time..*11*

Fumbles *12*

USMC..*18*

The Word Arrives *21*

Locker Box Meeting *26*

The Greeter *34*

The Smoking Lamp Is Out......................................*37*

Glad..*45*

Flight Of The Flu *48*

A Focus On Eternity..*51*

Cathedral Park *53*

Trusting..*56*

A Day At The Lake *61*

Ol' Blue...*67*

Rejoicing Together *71*

Cherry Strudel *75*

Gifts From The Sea...*79*

An Amazing Encounter...*84*

Words In Season..*90*

A Rushing Stream *93*

Strolling Onward *96*

It's Good *102*

Reaching Out *106*

What I Think *113*

Introduction

Life goes on, day by day. Things happen. Many of those things are ignored and forgotten. That is good. How could we survive remembering every little aspect of our lives?

Sometimes special things happen. They are different enough to be remembered. They are important enough to be remembered again and again. They are rewarding enough to be reviewed in our minds and in our hearts, day after day, year after year.

Chief among those important things are those very special times when God intervenes in our daily life. These are not times when we simply say, "Wow, God is good!" These are times when the movement of the Lord is so prominent as to be beyond overlooking. These are times a grateful heart must remember forever.

These are times to not only praise Him and rejoice in His care and presence, but to set up a living memorial testifying of His great love and attention. How can we fulfill Psalm 100:4,

> **"Enter into His gates with thanksgiving,**
> **and into His courts with praise;**
> **be thankful unto Him**
> **and bless His name."**

if we have forgotten all His gifts?

I remember when God pierced the veil that separates this world from eternity. He entered into my needs, my circumstances, my whereabouts, to give me a special glimpse of His dominion. One such occasion would have been a wonderful gift. The series of such times, spread throughout my life, make a great river of wonderful gifts. They make up the foundational thread in my life.

Sometimes the true importance of an event can only be seen by peering backward through the telescope of time.

Here is a thread of a few such living memorials, set up in the course of this life.

Each of the occasions recited below is one about which I can say,

"I Remember When . . ."

Remembering them is easy, because each of them, in some way, changed my life. More exactly, it was the intervention of God that changed my life.

While it is with joy and appreciation that I share these private events, I invite you, the reader, to search your own life experience for occasions where the Lord of the Universe entered time and circumstances to intervene, to guide, to enhance your life. Write these instances boldly on the tablet of your memory so you will always be ready to bring forth that spiritual offering of Thanksgiving.

And remember, when God is telling the story, there is always more to the story.

A Real Song

I can't really remember the school year in which it happened. Things are a little blurry back around then. I think it was probably sometime in 1939 when I was in the latter part of the third grade, at School 20 in Buffalo, NY.

One thing I am very sure of is this: it was the first *real* song I ever learned in school. A *real* song is a song real people sing. It is a song that is not made up to be cute and just for kids. It is not some old nursery rhyme. It is *real* and it is *important*. It is a song for grown-ups and we little kids were being taught it too!

I knew it was important because the music teacher came and took our whole class to a separate room to study it. Other classes were there too. That had never happened before. No two ways about it, this was a special event. A lot of changes took place in my life because of that one special event.

For one thing, I felt like a *real* person, the way a grown-up must feel. Here was something real being given to me, a little kid. I must say it again: This was a *real* song!

The song was about America. I only had a vague notion about what America was, but from this song I learned some wonderful things about being an American and being proud of my country and caring

3

about it. I even learned that a person could love their country and be excited about it and sing about it. That song planted a sense of patriotism deep within me. America was my home.

We were still in depression years. People thought they were well off if they had enough food for the family and money to pay the rent. Travel for the sake of pleasure was a mostly a foreign thought. I don't think I had ever even heard of the notion before. Who could afford to do that.? I invented it all by myself when I heard that song and came to understand its words. The goal of my life became to see the mountains and the prairies and the oceans, white with foam. That one song inspired in me a lifelong desire to see first one part, then another part of this beautiful country.

The song was important in another way. It was perhaps my first exposure to the word "God" as something other than a portion of a compound word used in times of anger or pain. I discovered that God could bless. You could talk to Him and ask him to take care of something as important and wonderful as your country. You could ask Him to stand by her side and guide her in whatever she needed guiding in. He even had some kind of special light that came from some place above, so He could even take care of her in the darkness of night.

Yes, I learned a lot that day, enough to last a life time: person-hood, patriotism, pursuit of beauty, and the presence of God. I didn't learn a lot about Him. I didn't learn His names. I didn't learn that He loved

me personally. I didn't even learn about sin. But I
did learn, deep inside someplace, that God IS. The
song, of course, was -

GOD BLESS AMERICA

God bless America, Land that I love.
Stand beside her and guide her,
Through the night with the light from above.
From the mountains, to the prairies,
To the oceans, white with foam,
God bless America, my home sweet home.
God bless America, my home sweet home.

And so, the journey began. The Holy Spirit that
Jesus promised would draw all men began His
drawing of this little man. Oh, he was a young man
and quite unaware of the nature of God. He was
still a child in knee pants, but he heard the call, he
began to respond, to receive, to rejoice.

I Remember When . . .

NOTE:

Irving Berlin wrote this song in 1939. Kate Smith first sang it that same year. I lived at 321 Crowley Avenue and attended School 20. That summer, we moved to 2009 Niagara Street and in the fall I started fourth grade at School 51.

I remember when God sent me to a special school assembly to learn about Him and His gift to me - America.

Call Of The Radio

Then came the early war years, 1942 or so. For me, they were filled with new and strange experiences. But there was always the comfort of home.

Sunday mornings were pleasant times. Six days of the week, Dad worked at the steel mill, but on Sundays he was home all day. Mom and he happily enjoyed being together. In my child's-eye view, these were comfortable times.

Each Sunday morning was almost like a holiday. Mom made a big breakfast for the three of us and Dad drank fresh brewed coffee from his oversize enameled steel mug. The smell of the coffee, the sound of Dad stirring that metal mug, the evident camaraderie between my parents, these are good and pleasant memories.

In the City of Buffalo, where I grew up, there were many neighborhoods that were more or less ethnic. These were places where immigrants of some national heritage lived together. There, they shared their old culture, their old language and their new dreams. Some of these areas were small and tight, just a block or two in size. Some were massive, covering a whole area of the city. Some even had their own weekly or monthly newspaper.

One outgrowth of this was that several of the local radio stations tried to build listener-ship by having special Sunday morning broadcasts. They had foreign language speaking hosts playing ethnic music. There were programs for the Germans and

I Remember When . . .

the Polish and the Italians and the Irish and the Hungarians and others. Buffalo was a multi-cultural city.

Because of their Hungarian birthright, my Mom and Dad were very keen to hear these programs. Much attention was focused on scanning the dial of the kitchen radio, looking for the right station and the right program. Probably because of careful planning, no two stations aired the same language at the same time. You could listen to one Hungarian program, then switch to another station to catch the next one. When the half hour struck, everything else in the house could wait, lest a favorite program be missed. There was much satisfaction in finding the right place on the dial. There was also much distress and anxious comment, and dialing back and forth, back and forth, when for some reason the program being sought did not show up as expected. Actual anger could erupt from such disappointment.

This radio ritual was a special pleasure in another way. We had not always had a working radio in our home. There was the big old Bosch floor model that stood in the living room. It dated back to before the time the Great Depression had begun. But, it had stopped working years before. There was no money to have it fixed. Yet, it was a fine piece of furniture and a remembrance of better times. Eventually, Ma had found a local merchant who would let us take home a new table model radio and pay for it bit by bit, a small payment each week.

I remember the trips to the jewelry store in Riverside, perhaps a mile from our house. Every week I would go with my mother and she would make the required payment. Often the two of us would walk there. I don't remember the exact amount any more, but it was very little by today's standards, perhaps only 75 cents a week. That seems incredibly small today, but even that was a challenge to the family finances. In that era my Dad's weekly take home pay was only about $30.00. But, the ability to meet this challenge, to have this prized possession, to again be able to hear voices from the outside world, just made those Sunday music programs more savory.

And so my folks listened, sometimes sang with the music, often talked back to the announcer, and enjoyed a wonderful family Sunday morning. I just watched and absorbed. I was outside the loop. I didn't speak Hungarian. I didn't have a personal experience with their music. I was just happy when things worked out well and they could be happy.

Also, there was a small technical aspect to this scene. Unless one has manually turned the dial of a radio, rather than using some modern electronic push-button means, they have not experienced the dynamic cacophony of sound generated as the unwanted stations whiz by. It is a staccato flood of meaningless noise. It is meaningless because you only hear it for an instant. It is noise because it is not what you are looking for. You just have to twist, twist, twist the dial to get the pointer over to the right number for the new station you want. And of course, since you are urgently looking for something, it is unthinkable that you would ever stop, even for a moment, and listen to one of these in-between stations and see what they have to offer.

Of course, in those days, and even later, I was not allowed to touch the prized possession. It would have been too dangerous to let a ten or eleven year old manipulate the dials. He might knock the whole radio to the floor and break it, and then where would we be? No! I could listen but not touch. And listen I did. I listened to the Hungarian music. I also listened to the Polish music and the German music, when it was allowed in. I listened to whatever my parents listened to. Later in the day I listened to Jack Benny and Eddie Cantor. I listened to Edgar Bergen and Charlie McCarthy.

But, I always yearned to listen to something else, something denied me. It was "that other music": those momentary flashes that passed by during the Sunday Morning scurrying back and forth across the dial. I didn't know what kind of music it was. I didn't know where it came from. I didn't know if it too represented some national group. All I knew was that I was drawn to it. It rang some kind of bell inside me. I desired it. How I wished my folks would stop some time on one of those stations, so I could hear "That Other Music." But they never did and I didn't have a vote. And years passed and I forgot all about the tugging and yearning I had felt.

Then, one day, two decades later, I heard "That Other Music" again. I recognized it at once. It wasn't on the radio, that I heard it. It was in a Pentecostal church. It was God's music, praising Him! Yes, even as a child of 10 or so, the Holy Spirit had been quickening my spirit by anointing the tiniest fragments of praise to God.

I remember when God, again and again, used tiny fragments of radio music to inspire a desire in my being to enter into worship.

Lunch Time

I suppose the year should be 1942 or so. In those days I attended a neighborhood school, just a few blocks from home. We were released for lunch time. Although there was a school cafeteria, most students didn't use it. Most of us walked home for lunch. Then we walked back to school for the afternoon session.

Coming home for lunch on Gorton Street, I regularly found the radio on. Often, as I arrived, it was saying, "It's high noon. Here is Kate Smith." Kate Smith sang a variety of songs and a segment of the program brought the news of the day, usually war news. Intermingling with the other songs were spiritual songs, songs that recognized God, and His sovereignty, and His love. They created an impression on my mind, my heart, my understanding, an orientation, an acceptability of God.

This was cast in an atmosphere of love, because my mother was always glad to see me home from school. She was busy, seeing to it that my lunch was ready on schedule, so I could get out of there and get back to school on time. She was caring for me, pleasantly, and Kate Smith was singing, "May The Good Lord Bless and keep You."

I remember when God sent Kate Smith into our kitchen at noontime, five days a week, to tell me that God is and God loves.

Fumbles

One main task of adolescence is to learn how to take charge of one's own world, one's life. In those ancient days when I was an adolescent, a main thrust to that search for control was to discover how to stay out of trouble: at home, at school, on the street.

That's not easy when you're a young person. You don't yet know all the active elements in each situation you meet. Strange things happen when you least expect them. What you learned last week and what gave you confidence for this week's encounters may prove to be totally insufficient. Whamo! Behind the old eight-ball again!

At least that was my experience. Large parts of my high school years were spent in planning, analyzing and agonizing over how to conduct day-to-day activities in a safe and productive way. I believed that what I didn't know I could figure out from things that I did know or from careful observation. Another thing was to plan everything in advance, down to the last syllable. But there were failures, nonetheless. And the failures led to even more introspection. After a while, some principles began to emerge.

Actually, I now realize that the attitudes evolved before the principles were understood and identified. The attitudes came out of the fire of my own life experiences and my observation of the experiences of others. I know one of the things that helped form those attitudes was Rudyard Kipling's timeless poem, "IF." I came into possession of it in a way that was unconventional, but for our post-depression days, fairly typical. Someone in the neighborhood was discarding some old belongings. They were put out on the curb awaiting the trash pickup. We scooped them up. There were several good picture frames we might be able to use some time and a few other things.

One of the picture frames had this poem in it. It was lettered in some kind of fancy script with flowers all around it. The glass front had kept it from being damaged. I cleaned it up and hung it in my room. Once or twice a year I dusted it and read it again. It always seemed like something important to me, but it was so long I couldn't seem to grasp the whole thing. Nonetheless, I gathered the general implications and I guess they penetrated into my heart and mind. Here is what the poem said:

I Remember When . . .

IF

If you can keep your head when all about you
  Are losing theirs, and blaming it on you,
If you can trust yourself when all men doubt you,
  But make allowance for their doubting too;
If you can wait and not be tired by waiting,
  Or being lied about, don't deal in lies,
  Or being hated, don't give way to hating,
  And yet don't look too good nor talk too wise. . .
If you can dream and not make dreams your master,
If you can think, and not make thoughts your aim,
If you can meet with triumph and disaster,
  And treat those two imposters just the same;
If you can bear to hear the truth you've spoken
  Twisted by knaves to make a trap for fools,
  Or watch the things you gave your life to, broken,
  And stoop and build 'em up with worn-out tools;
If you can make one heap of all your winnings,
  And risk it on one turn of pitch-and toss,
  And lose, and start again at your beginnings,
  And never breathe a word about your loss. . .
If you can force your heart and nerve and sinew
  To serve your turn long after they are gone,
  And so hold on when there is nothing in you
  Except the will which says to them: "Hold on!"
If you can walk with kings-nor lose the common touch,
If neither foes nor loving friends can hurt you,
If all men count with you, but none too much;
If you can fill the unforgiving minute
  With sixty seconds' worth of distance run,
  Yours is the Earth and everything that's in it,
  And - - which is more - -
        You'll be a Man, my Son!

Rudyard Kipling

14

In time, I wanted to put into writing some of the things I had discovered. I wanted to create simple, direct, concise statements that anyone could understand at the first reading. You, see, I wanted to write something that would communicate to others that which I saw as my attained wisdom.

At the same time, I was much too insecure to ever let anyone know I had even thought such things, let alone written them. I was an adolescent.

One of the principles I set down on paper was this:

"It's not the fumble that counts, but the recovery."

Perhaps you can see a fine thread of relationship dangling out of the poem, "IF", when you read my statement. I was a little proud of being able to use a sports vernacular to express this thought, even though I was never active in sports myself. I thought the terms were some nearly anyone would understand, and that was my main goal in crafting the formal expression of this principle.

The idea was that mistakes *will* happen, things *will* go wrong, plans *will* fail. Plan on it, expect it, be prepared for it. That is the way of life. Not everything goes wrong. To believe that would be foolishly pessimistic. But things do go wrong. To ignore that would be worse than being foolish.

My idea was that the things that go wrong are not important to me because I have no control over them. I have done my conscientious best and they went wrong anyway. What **IS** important is what I do after: after the mistake, after the wrong, after the failure.

Some of this insight came about as a result of my fledgling efforts in mechanics and wood craft. I had no end of failures, but none that could not be fixed with enough perseverance and patience. I became a person who was always willing to start from where I was, rather than lament about not being where I had sought to be.

It was a broader vision than simply not "crying over spilt milk." It included that, but it also required cleaning up the mess and replacing the lost milk. The attitude that ignores the fumble (except to learn from it) but squarely faces the task of recovery has served me well all these decades since I first wrote those words. The most important benefit I got from my motto was that fear of the result evaporated. I was now willing to try things, to be adventuresome, to apply my knowledge and see what the result would be.

*"It's not the fumble that counts,
but the recovery."*

Once many years later, I was thrilled to hear my Pastor proclaim the exact same truth. He has a facility with words that far surpasses that shown in that simple phrase I had written, years before he was born.

It was a joy to hear the old principle proclaimed.

It was a delight to hear it expounded, illuminated, and delivered to hundreds of others.

This is what he said on November 26,1995:

"Failure does not disqualify you.
Your history does not dictate your destiny.
What you haven't yet accomplished
    does not determine
    what you're going to be.
It's what you do with failure.
Failure is not defeat.

The Scripture says that
    A righteous man,
    A just man,
    A devout man,
    A man that serves God,
    He falls seven times
        and he gets back up again."

I remember when, years earlier, by a discarded poem and the whispering of His Holy Spirit, God had taught me this scriptural principle. He did it at a time when I didn't even know such things existed. He met my needs before I knew Him or His Word.

USMC

It was the time of the Korean war. Young men were being called into the armed forces. I had been a college student and, as such, had been deferred from the draft. But when it came time to enroll for the 1951 Fall semester, personal circumstances had made it impossible. While the cost was tiny by today's measure, I didn't have it. Education loans and grants hadn't been invented yet. Instead of returning to the University of Buffalo, I just continued to work at my job.

In due time, I received the letter I knew must come. I was to report for induction. It was not something I wanted to do, but of course I had no real choice. To the Army I must go for two years.

On a cold Buffalo morning in February of 1952, I reported to the induction center with about a hundred other young men. We moved in a steady stream from room to room, answering questions and filling out forms. Part of this process was a physical examination to make an initial determination of our suitability for military service. Being able to walk from room to room seemed to be sufficient evidence. As I entered one area, a Sergeant was seated facing me across a desk. He seized the papers from my hand, shuffled them until he found the right page, glanced at me quickly, then filled in three blanks: hair - brown, eyes - brown, temperature - 98.6. Off to the next room.

At last, with all the paper work finished, we were gathered in a big room, all in a straight line, facing the center of the room.

An officer appeared. He explained that we were not all going to the Army. Some would be privileged to go to the Marine Corps. Those who stepped forward first, the first 20, would become United States Marines.

In most eras there would have been men anxious to become Marines. Not that day.

The Marine Corps did not draft men. The Army drafted men. Marines enlisted, for four years, of their own free will. However, this day Marines were being drafted. There was a reason for it and it hinged on tragedy.

The United States Marine Corps Recruit Depot at Parris Island, South Carolina was notorious as a furnace where listless young men were molded and refined into fighting machines, their very natures changed to be at once obedient and aggressive.

There is something revealing about the name of the place, in particular, the word "Depot." A training center is for people, but a depot is for things: equipment, supplies, resources. Marines in training were objects, to be modified for military use. Of course, I didn't understand this at the time. The reputation might have been enough to deter some who might otherwise volunteer, but there was more.

Recently a young recruit had died at Parris Island. He was the son of a prominent media personality. Needless to say, there was much questioning.

I Remember When . . .

Charges and denials rippled throughout the news media. Marine Corps boot camp had gotten a black eye. Now, on this day in February 1952, of the hundred or so men gathered at the induction center, not one volunteered for the Marine Corps.

Personally, I had no notion of what I ought to do. I had no basis for a decision, so I made no decision. As a matter of fact, since I had not chosen to be part of this at all, I determined to not participate in the decision of Army of Marines. I would not step out either.

Then it happened. The officer changed the name of the game. "Everyone who does NOT want to go in the Marine Corps, step back three paces." While I contemplated this sudden change in circumstances, dozens of young men quickly stepped backward. I was stuck with my decision to not move. I was now a Marine recruit.

By making no decision, I had indeed, made a far reaching decision. As I later understood, it wasn't my decision at all. It was God's. And I didn't even know Him yet! Oh, He could have used other ways to bless my life -- but He choose this way.

I remember when God locked my feet to the floor so He could lead me in His paths.

The Word Arrives

For the Word of God
is quick, and powerful,
and sharper than any two edged sword,
piercing even to the dividing asunder
of soul and spirit,
and of the joints and marrow,
and is a discerner of
the thoughts and intents of the heart.
<u>Heb 4:12</u>

But I had never heard this word! I had not seen it. I knew in only a vague way that it existed – some place.

In my early days, my grandparents on both sides of the family were alive. In those days children were to be "seen and not heard." And it was so with me. So, my interaction with them was limited. None of them practiced a saving faith as far as I could tell. Belief in the Lord of Lords was not a part of their daily life.

It was the same with my parents. They were all good people, usually moral and upright. Perhaps because of their family backgrounds and some childhood experiences, my parents avoided the institution of church and all that went with it. And so, I remained untaught, un-discipled, and unsaved.

I Remember When . . .

The church-going people of our community were respected. There were a number of churches of different denominations in our little neighborhood. They were respected, but avoided. We celebrated Christmas and Easter with gifts and special food. But God was never invited.

Most of what I knew I learned from the radio or in school. In those days, during the Christmas season, the radio played the old Christmas Carols: Silent Night, Come All Ye Faithful, Oh Little Town Of Bethlehem and such. (Rudolf the Red Nosed Reindeer was yet to be born but I think Frosty The Snowman was already on the scene.)

Much insight could be harvested from these songs. They portrayed a whole world that I had no other knowledge of. Music class in school gave me a chance to see those words in print, not just hear them. There was even a booklet of Christmas songs you could have to keep. It was provided free by the Prudential Insurance Company.

So, I came to know a little about the Christmas story and a little less about the Easter story. Years rushed by and I became a young adult. With that came some new responsibilities. There was a war going on in Korea and I wound up in the United States Marine Corps.

Anyone who has ever followed that path knows some things about boot camp. It is long. It is oppressive. Much time is spent standing in lines waiting for the next thing to happen. There is no freedom. No personal reading materials such as newspapers, magazines or books are allowed.

Reading was limited to two and only two documents: The Marine Corps Manual and the Holy Bible. The Marine Corps manual was supplied.

Just about the first thing to happen at the boot camp at Parris Island, SC, was the great clothing transfer. The powers that be saw to it that we surrendered all our civilian clothing to be mailed home. Our prior identity was history. Then we were led though a maze of stacks from which we each gathered our new supplies: shirts and socks, trousers and caps, boots and toiletries, etc. etc.

Tired, laden down with new gear, in doubt about what would come next, we reached the end of the winding line and approached the exit door into the outside world.

There, near that door, was a small square table. On the table was a small stack of books. There was a sign that said "Free." Haltingly, I took one, mostly because I didn't know I didn't have to. It turned out to be a pocket size copy of the New Testament made available by the American Bible Society.

The book was small enough to be unobvious in my boot camp uniform. It went wherever I went. When the flow of activity allowed, I would pull it out and read it. In our "Hurry up and wait" environment there was nothing else to do anyway.

Having never owned a copy of the Bible before, I was curious. I began reading at the front of the book. After all, that's what you do with a book, right? I didn't have an advisor to send me to some other portion first.

I found the book of Matthew to be very interesting. It tied together a lot of the things I had gleaned from those school songs. They made more and more sense to me. Christmas and Easter took on new meaning for me. I began to understand who this Jesus person was. I was glad to have this little book. I was glad to have time to read it too.

Then I went on to the book of Mark. Huh! I was not all that taken with Mark. A lot of it seemed to be the same story I had just read in Matthew. I wondered if the whole volume would be one repetition after another. In any case, I read on, picking up one insight here and another there. There was enough gain to keep me going.

Then, of course, I went on to the book of Luke. Oh My! More yet. Yet, somehow, I read even more avidly. There was a strange attraction in these lines. I began to assent. I began to agree. I began to see that Jesus was for me and that I needed Him. Then, suddenly, it was finished. Some place in the book of Luke, I believed! Having believed, I repented. I was saved. I was born again.

Oh, I didn't understand. Over 62 years have passed and I still don't understand all I would like to. But these things I know: Jesus is the Christ, the risen Lord, the Creator and Sustainer of the universe, the Redeemer of my sinful soul, and the One who loves me as a brother.

Months later, I visited my home town of Buffalo on leave. It looked so different to me. It was bright and shining and I felt an inward joy as I beheld it. Oh, the city had not changed during my absence – but the eye of the beholder had undergone a new birth.

Many years followed, many bibles of different sizes and translations. Reference books came into use. At times I became a teacher of others.

I remember when God saw a needy youth, put into his hands a copy of the New Testament, and sequestered him in a Marine Corp boot camp long enough to find time to read through Matthew, Mark and part of Luke. How remarkable!

Locker Box Meeting

Holidays are strange times when you are far from home and alone.

When the holiday is New Years Day, it is especially peculiar. New Year's Day is usually a time for taking stock of the year just passed, and perhaps of all the other past years. It is also a time to look ahead and anticipate the future, the prospects and the threats that it holds.

Never has a holiday been more peculiar for me than the day 1954 began. I was alone in my barracks building at Camp LeJeune, North Carolina. I mean alone! Of the 80 or so men that normally occupied that huge cavern of a room, I was the only one there. All the others had dispersed to far places for the holidays. I was alone and lonely. My loneliness didn't come just from being alone in the building. It came from being alone in the world.

It was the middle of the day and I was sitting on my wooden locker box at the side of my bunk. If you have ever been in the military, you know there is no place else to sit in a barracks building. There are no chairs or couches or tables. There are only lockers, bunks and, slid under the bunks, locker boxes.

The barracks are where you sleep and where you keep your personal belongings. It is not intended that you spend much time there otherwise. There are always plenty of work activities to keep you busy elsewhere. But of course, holidays are different. It was quiet in the barracks that day. Everyone else in my Company had found some other place to be for these days. I had decided to "tough it out." My locker box was my home. It held my few treasures as well as my clothes. It was MY place in the Marine Corps. As I sat there, I contemplated the future, a suitable exercise for New Year's Day.

In another six weeks my tour of duty in the United States Marine Corps would end. Life would change, but to what?

I was determined to use this day, this time, this solitude, to find some answer, any answer. I had set this time apart for this purpose. And so, alone on that locker box, I began to pray. It was only about a year and half since I had found out about Jesus and accepted His invitation. I had been faithful in attending church, wherever the Marine Corps had located me: South Carolina, North Carolina, Great Lakes, San Diego, North Carolina again. I had even read some more of the Bible. Now I needed His help -- really! "Lord, what will become of me?"

I sat there taking inventory of my life: "Who am I? What can I do to earn a living? Where?" I owned nothing but the things in the locker box: no car, no civilian wardrobe, no bank account, no job. That was the real reason for my feelings of loneliness!

I mentally reviewed my prior jobs, my skills and my education. My time in college had lacked the direction it needed. Three years there had really not prepared me for anything of value. The old goals, such as they were, no longer seemed important. New goals did not exist.

I Remember When . . .

Whatever stream of life I had been part of before the Marine Corps had certainly flowed on without me. That stream was gone and gone for good. A few recent attempts at communicating with some old acquaintances had proven that. Somehow, I was going to have to start a whole new life.

These thoughts, these feelings, had been in the background of my mind for some time. This day, they came to the foreground with full force. Alone, facing a new year, about to be released and turned loose on my own, I felt the seriousness of my situation. My view of my future looked absolutely blank: not dark, but blank.

The Marine Corps had trained me to repair a few specific models of their two-way field radios. Those radios were already obsolete. There was no future there.

I tried a brain-storming approach. Forget the income. Forget the location. Forget what I know or don't know. Focus on one thing: what would I like to do as a daily activity? Don't think about titles and designations. Think about the actual, active, moment by moment doing. Get down to the detail level. Hope to work back from there to some meaningful profession or trade. Anything. . . . Nothing!

This was a focused time. I put everything else out of my mind but God and my question. I just sat there, wondering in God's presence. Then something happened that I really didn't expect. (Being a relatively new Christian, I guess I didn't know what to expect.) After a while, He gave me a visualization of an activity. What I saw immediately intrigued me. It captured my mind and my enthusiasm. It was pleasing to me. I was sure it was something I could do. Even more, I knew it was something I would like doing. Why, it almost seemed familiar, but of course it couldn't be.

Even today, decades later, I cannot well describe the visualization I received that New Year's day in 1954. It involved things that I did not know existed at the time. The closest I can come is to speak of problem solving, of analysis, of dealing with intricate things, be they mechanical, electrical, electronic or organizational.

It somehow involved seeing things as they would be if they were the way they should be. It seemed to hinge on some kind of beauty that can be seen in order, in function, in completeness.

I had no idea where the activities of the visualization could be practiced, or for what purpose, or how to obtain the opportunity, or who would be willing to pay for my services. Nonetheless, the peace I sought had come. The worry had changed to waiting to see what God would do. I now knew that somewhere within me was an ability that would be valuable someplace and that God would lead me to that place. I just knew it!

My peace in the matter became so complete that I spent no more time thinking on the subject. The six weeks passed, I was discharged from the Marine Corps, I took the long bus ride home to Buffalo and once again occupied my old room in my parents home on Gorton Street.

I Remember When . . .

Shortly, I began to look for work. I was not too aggressive, mostly because I didn't know how to effectively go about the matter. It's hard to look for work when you don't know what kind of work to look for or where to look for it.

My general plan was to return to college in the Fall of the year and complete what I had started years earlier. I had no real college goal. It was just that I had always felt compelled to complete anything I had started, and I had not yet completed college. In the mean time, I would need to earn some money to meet current expenses and to pay for college. In my view, I needed a job for the summer.

One day I found something interesting in the classified columns of the local newspaper. The notice did not give the name of the employer, only the name of an employment agency. That bothered me a little. I wanted to know more about what I was getting into. However, they offered to provide training, on the job and in their own schools. Salary, benefits and expenses would be paid during the training. Also, they had a preference for people who had been trained in electronics in the military. That was me.

"Something" told me to check this out, <u>quickly</u>.

The next morning, I was at the employment agency 15 minutes before they opened. The lady that opened the office was very helpful. She took some information and sent me directly to a place just a few blocks away on Delaware Avenue. She made it a point to tell me to go immediately and that this company almost never advertised or used

30

employment agencies. They preferred to do their own recruiting.

When I arrived, they were expecting me. I was given a quick tour of the office and the repair shop. I was shown equipment the likes of which I had never imagined. Next, came a 45 minute written exam, dealing with principles of physics and electricity. I had known all these things since high school. I remembered them well since they were so interesting to me. The interviewer smiled and remarked on how well I had done. I was encouraged. Then he disappointed me by saying they would have to check my references and they would let me know if they had a position for me. I went home to wait.

A month passed. During that month I did no more job hunting. I spent two weeks in bed with a sore throat and the flu, no doubt a supplemental benefit of moving from North Carolina to Buffalo in February.

Also, during that month, my grandmother took me shopping for a car. We picked out a black 1950 four-door Chrysler sedan that she paid for with $1000 cash out of her pocket book. I was to repay it in installments, no interest, when I got a job.

During this time I also heard that someone had been in the neighborhood asking questions about me.

One morning the telephone rang. It was for me. It was someone from IBM. They wanted to tell me that I had been accepted as an employee and they wanted to know when I would like to start.

"When would I like to start? You're asking me, not telling me? Wow!"

As I recall, it was a Tuesday when they called and I selected the following Monday, April 25th 1954 to be my start date. The company was the International Business Machines Corporation and I became an IBM Customer Engineer, a CE.

For the first few weeks, I tagged along with an experienced CE as he went from account to account fixing machines and meeting customers' needs. Then I went to school for ten weeks in Endicott, New York and learned all about the equipment that manipulated punch cards. When I returned, I was assigned my own territory and went to work.

Later I was sent to a school in Poughkeepsie to learn some things about computers. This yielded me a transfer to Schenectady where I met my wife-to-be.

It was nearly thirty-three years before I retired from what I had expected to be a summer job. (The interviewer had not asked if I was looking for permanent employment and it had not occurred to me to tell him otherwise. Good thing!) In all those years, although I had many different titles and worked in different cities at various tasks, that one view, granted me on a locker box, never failed.

It's taking a lifetime to understand the fullness of it, but there can be no doubt that God had known the end, known it before the beginning. He knew my skills and abilities. After all, He placed them in me. As we met on that New Year's Day, He had shared with me just that amount that I was able to understand. The things on which I worked in the latter thirty years of my IBM career had not even existed on the day I sat on my locker box. The avalanche of technology that was to include the electronic computer, transistors, integrated circuits and a huge array of other things was poised on the time-line of the future, about to make its first tiny motions.

Only God could have foreseen my role in that great flow.

By the way, I only applied for one job when I came home from the Marine Corps. The newspaper ad described my personal training as a requirement. Everything else I would need was to be provided.

I remember when God opened the door to a career for which He had already prepared me and blessed all my future years.

The Greeter

Sunday morning church was a standard event for our family. Sunday School for the kids was too. We attended the services of one of the mainline denominations. We were known and involved. The word that was preached was Biblical. Sometimes it was interesting and challenging.

In the course of time, some friends invited us to go with them to a special evening service at another church. They themselves would be guests of someone who attended regularly. A special guest from out of town would present the program that evening, someone that was well received on a prior visit. We talked it over and decided to go. Sunday evening church was not part of our practice, but our friends seemed enthusiastic.

The evening began with a time of worship in song. My, how these people could sing! So much gusto! It was as if the God they were worshipping was right there with them. We were at once caught up in that outpouring of praise. Somehow, I could once again hear those tiny snippets of music from that radio station that beckoned me so long ago.

The whole family seemed to enjoy the experience and to want more. Soon we went back for some other Sunday night services. We became more or less regulars on Sunday evenings.

It became evident that we liked the new place better that the old place. We felt closer to God there. The preaching was dynamic and sure. The music was worshipful and joyous. I often felt the desire to raise my eyes along with my voice as I sang out with the congregation. I wanted to praise God, not hide from Him. We felt He lifted our hearts whenever we went. We began to consider going there on Sunday mornings.

But there was a problem. We had heard some odd reports about this church and its doctrine. We heard they didn't approve of smoking. I smoked. We heard they didn't approve of the use of alcohol. I drank a bit occasionally. And there were some other things we didn't understand too.

Was the Sunday night service just a special casual program, calculated to be attractive and disarming, and was Sunday morning, the real church, something totally different, strict, managed, strange?. Clearly a decision had to be made. In time, I did something I had never done before: I took command of the spiritual life of my household.

The next Sunday morning the family stayed home. I went to the new church, alone. I was on a mission to seek out blessing and to avoid any thing that perhaps should be avoided. I was going to investigate the Sunday morning service. I know it sounds odd. It may even sound preposterous. But that was my mission.

I arrived at the appointed time. It was Summer and the wide doors at the front of the church stood propped open. As I climbed the few stairs to the doorway my mind was alert. "Watch for strangeness."

I reached the doorway. I stepped across the threshold. In that instant the most amazing thing that had ever happened in my life took place. The Holy Spirit of God welcomed me!

He enveloped me with His presence. His peace overflowed me. I felt as if I had come to my home, my home where I had never been before, but my home.

No usher had yet greeted me. No Pastor had shaken my hand. No songs had been sung. No message had been preached. God Himself, in the manifestation of His Holy Spirit, greeted me. I understood at once that it was OK.

What is more, not only were my doubt and protective stance on behalf of my family acceptable, they were approved.

Later I learned about being the priest of my home.

So, we all, my family, and friends I gathered from time to time, came regularly, often three times a week, to the church where the Holy Spirit had greeted me in person.

I remember when God met me at the threshold of the place where I was seeking Him and said to my entire being,

"Welcome, I am here."

The Smoking Lamp Is Out

They were fine folk.
They were friendly folk.
They were upstanding, moral, and loving folk.
They loved Jesus and they loved those that Jesus loved.
That included me.

Long before I met them, I had been covered by the blood of Jesus. But I had little or no understanding of what it all meant. As a matter of fact, I had drifted somewhat from the principles of life I had affirmed when I first read the New Testament several years earlier.

Now I was a family man, attending a church that was new to me. I enjoyed the gospel music and the teaching and I felt uplifted at every service.

For years I had smoked tobacco in one form or another. Dad always smoked cigarettes. In the depression days of my youth, they were always the cheapest cigarettes available. Nonetheless, they were a staple item of the weekly budget that he and mom worked out each Saturday morning.

When I first smoked, in high school, it was cigarettes I smoked. They tasted harsh, the smoke hurt my eyes, the smell was without any attraction, but I smoked. Why? I don't know. I didn't know then and I don't know now. Perhaps it had something to do with the thrill of avoiding detection, for my parents would certainly not have approved. I do know that it was in keeping with the Biblical principle that

37

proclaims that the life attributes of the parents will be manifested in the lives of their offspring for generations to come.

Later, I began to smoke pipes. They provided a more pleasant aroma, and they came in interesting shapes. Pipes were more bothersome than cigarettes, but more satisfying. Eventually, I had a collection of nearly 30 pipes, of which three or four were special favorites, some even from college days.

When I was a young child my father's parents were still alive. Once or twice a summer there would be a special holiday. We would all take a day trip together in the old family car. Perhaps we would go to a state park. Perhaps to some old-country friends living on a farm. Dad would drive and mom would sit up front with him. His parents and I would squeeze together in the back seat. Fortunately, I was always placed near a window so I could see out. (This was the family remedy for the threat of car sickness.)

Since I did not speak their language and they did not speak mine, I had no direct communications with my grandparents. Somehow, even the few English words I directed at them from time to time came out sounding disrespectful and too familiar in their ears.

These trips were very special occasions for my grandparents. Of course, they had no automobile. Many Americans didn't in the late 1930's. Since their command of the English language was so slight, most public transportation was also beyond their comfortable use. Besides, they had no funds for casual travel. So, unless someone with an automobile gathered them up for an excursion, they went nowhere.

In recognition of these special times, my grandmother and grandfather would wear their nicest clothes, fitting to the royal nature of the day. These were the years before air conditioning. Yet, there would be my grandfather beside me in the back seat of the car in midsummer. Suit, vest, necktie, golden watch chain, fedora or derby - and a brand new cigar, freshly lit just after entering the car.

The lighting of that cigar was absolutely ceremonial. When everyone was in the car, still fussing a little about the lay of their clothes and the positioning of their feet and whatever little items they had brought along, but before the car actually began to move, out would come the cigar from its vest pocket domicile. A little examination, careful placement in the mouth, a book of matches from another vest pocket, puff, puff, puff, aah! His was a really aristocratic experience on these special days.

At once, my grandmother and I were engulfed in smoke. It sounds terrible. It sounds punishing. But I loved it. The family was together. Holiday was happening. I was enjoying the only relationship I had with my grandfather, sharing the back seat with him and his cigar.

And the cigar was very aromatic. And I loved "aromatic." It was the aroma that made pipe-smoking appealing to me later in my life. Many years later, when the responsibilities of my employment made it inconvenient to smoke a pipe, the transition to cigars was very easy.

I Remember When . . .

Smoking cigars became a full time business with me. I smoked them continually. I bought them by the boxes, mail order, 150 or so cigars at a time. I always had a box of cigars in the bottom drawer of my desk at work. I kept another box under the driver's seat of my van. A third box stayed in my wood working shop in the basement where I spent a lot of my evening hours.

At the start of the day I had a standard routine: get in the van, start the engine, reach under the seat, get a cigar, light it, fasten the seat belt, put the van in gear, depart.

At the end of the day I had another routine: walk through the house checking that the various outside doors were locked, shut off the lights as I went, stop last in the den, place my still lighted cigar in the ashtray, shut off that light, go to my room and to bed.

Even at lunch, the cigar had a role. As I went through the cafeteria line with my friends, a cigar was still in my mouth. When we reached our table, I put down the tray, sat in my seat, moved the cigar from my lips to the ashtray, and began to eat. When I had finished eating, the cigar went at once from the ash tray to my mouth. Often, it was still burning.

I never went anywhere without a cigar in my mouth and at least two or three more in the breast pocket of my suit coat. There was a vague sense of insecurity if the pocket got down to only one "spare." Things continued in this way for years.

And so, in the fullness of time, I began to attend the new church. On a Sunday morning, I would go up the driveway of the church puffing on my cigar. After the car was parked and the whole family was out, I would take one more puff and carefully place my cigar in the ashtray for later. No use wasting the balance of a good cigar!

Of course, the "spares" were in my coat pocket. They were prominent, a symbol of security and affluence, just as they were to my grandfather at those holiday times.

The people at the new church didn't smoke. They regarded it as a form of bondage and perhaps a sin. They would greet me with much friendliness and sincerity. Invariably, their eye would flick to my breast pocket and back as they took note of the hateful objects residing there. But their smiles never failed and no one ever said a word to me about smoking.

(One time someone did remove my half-smoked cigar from my automobile ash tray during the service. I know they didn't smoke it. Perhaps they only wanted to destroy it - or maybe it became a tool for focused prayer on my behalf.)

Now, I enjoyed smoking cigars. I liked the taste - and when I didn't, I'd buy a package of some other brand and trade off for a while. And I saw nothing wrong with the whole thing. Of course, this was years before the Surgeon General's dire labels about the dangers of smoking.

Yet, Sunday after Sunday, there were friendly smiles and a flick of the eyes. The people were loving me, and checking on my progress, and hurt by my lack of it. My smoking was hurting them!

One bright Sunday morning, after the service, I strolled along the walk in front of the church and I spoke to God. "Look," I said, "I like to smoke, I enjoy it and I don't see anything wrong with it, but if you want it you can have it." It wasn't a very well framed prayer, but it was a genuine and personal communication with my God. I had yielded my cigars to Him. I remember almost nothing about the remainder of that day.

Early Monday I started out on the standard morning routine. Here's how it went: Get in the van, start the engine, reach under the seat, get out a cigar, light it, "Yeech! The sun must have gotten to these cigars. Awful taste. I'll wait to get a good one at work."

Here's how it went at work: walk to my office, sit in my chair, unlock my desk, open the bottom drawer, take out a cigar, light it, "Yeech! This whole shipment must be lousy." This was hard for me to understand since I had already smoked about a half of each box with no problem, but what other explanation could there be? I had no other idea.

By the time lunchtime arrived I was already about three cigars down for the day. Here it was almost 12 noon and I had not yet smoked my first cigar. I made a quick path to the drug store up the street from my office. They had one of these big humidors, about 5 feet high and 4 feet wide, with sliding glass doors, all just to keep expensive cigars humid and fresh. I selected a package of my very favorites, a little too expensive to smoke regularly, but always good when I felt I deserved a special treat for some reason or another. I certainly deserved a special treat today. Hadn't two boxes of cigars gone bad on me in just one morning?

I moved to the checkout counter, paid for the cigars, and walked out on the sidewalk in front of the store. There I stopped. Open the bag, rip the cellophane off the package, open the little cardboard box, remove one of the five special cigars waiting there, peel off its personal cellophane wrapper, light up, take a good puff, "Yeech!"

Yep! You guessed it. These cigars tasted awful too. After three "bad" cigars in such a short part of the day, I really didn't have a lot of desire to try any more. Not for the rest of the day. Nor the next day. Nor the next year nor the next decade.

The taste was gone, the desire was gone, the insecurity was gone: the cigars were gone.

Here is perhaps the strangest part of this story: I didn't have the vaguest notion of what had happened. I just knew I didn't smoke anymore. I didn't have to check my pockets before leaving my office anymore. No lighter weighing down my jacket pocket. And I didn't miss it. I thought, "This is strange, but heck, I'll save a couple bucks - and the folks at church will be happy."

Over a period of months it slowly dawned on me that God had taken away my dependence on tobacco - just like that. It had been sudden and complete. I hadn't even realized it was His work. I was just glad to be free of all the complications that went along with smoking.

Still later something else happened that completed my illumination regarding the matter. Again, I was on my way to work in the morning, a beautiful, bright, sunny day. I was praising God and reflecting on various teachings as I drove along. Suddenly I had a question I wanted an answer to. I had heard it said that "The Holy Spirit is a gentleman," meaning that He never forces you into anything. He may set the circumstances, but you yourself must voluntarily respond to them. God wants our yielding and our commitment. He is not in the business of forcing us. If He was, we would be only robots.

So I said, "God, how did that work? You just took away my smoking without my ever even asking you to. I don't understand."

Then, faster than you can say "revelation," I did understand. At that moment, into my mind popped the scene of that morning on the walk outside church. Instantly I understood the whole thing. I had not asked, I had not been forced, I had simply yielded. And now I was reminded.

Later I learned a little more about that. With God, yielding will do it every time. That is what He wants from us. He wants us to yield our hearts, our habits, our families, our finances, our very lives. He wants us to "let go and let Him."

I remember when God heard my simple prayer of yielding and responded by changing the very chemistry of my mouth so that I could be free from the effects of tobacco.

Glad

It happened week after week. Church was wonderful. The presence of God was glorious. People were friendly. Some were especially attractive: comely in the Biblical sense. There was just something special about greeting them. I was GLAD to see them. It was fun. I didn't think about it a lot. I just knew that the Lord is God and I trusted in Him.

Then one day, as I was reading the Word, I suddenly understood. David knew all about it. He knew what I was experiencing. He spoke in the future tense, but he must already have had a glimmer of experience. Here is what David said

"They that fear thee will be GLAD when they see me; because I have hoped in thy Word."
(Psalm 119:74.)

It was as if the comely people of God were saying –

    "They that fear thee..."
        That's me, I'm the "they" to them.

    "...will be GLAD..."
        That's me again! I'm GLAD.

    "...when they see me..."
        People like David. That's you.

    "...because I have hoped in thy Word."
        You hope in His Word,
            and that makes me glad.

Now I understood. I had hoped in God's Word. These other people, the attractive ones, they too had hoped in God's Word. That's why I was always so GLAD to see them. That's why they were GLAD to see me.

It didn't matter that I didn't know anything else about them; that I didn't know about their jobs, or families, or background, or education, or trials, or victories; sometimes, not even their names. It was enough to know that they had hoped in the Word of God.

But, how could I possibly have found that out, not "knowing them?" How?

It was your Spirit, wasn't it Lord? Your Spirit in them bore witness to Your Spirit in me! And each of us became GLAD to see each other! What a wonderful gift. David understood it: It's hoping in God's Word that binds people together.

Then one day I found out that Charles Spurgeon, the great preacher and teacher of the past understood it also. When he read David's words in Psalm 119:74, he wrote this comment:

> "He who comes forth perfumed with the spices of God's word imparts delight to all with whom he associates."

Isn't that the truth! Aren't you delighted when you get to spend time with someone who has the perfume of God's word all over their life? It's hoping in God's Word that creates union. And it is a wonderful and precious gift.

But Lord, Somehow I'm lonely.

I'm GLAD when I see them, but I don't see them very much.

Our unity in your Spirit is great, but I'd like to have more than that.

Lord; remember when you made Adam? You wanted fellowship. I'd like to have fellowship too. I'd like to know the names and the jobs and the needs and the victories. I'd like to be known.

But so many of your people who make me GLAD are too busy to be known. I guess you already know that. You must miss them too, huh?

Well, I see that You keep going after them and trying to be part of their lives. That's a good example. That's what I'm going to do.

Maybe just a breakfast or lunch together once in a while. You and I, we'll go after them together.

They might forget us sometimes, but we'll work to be there when they want us;

Because we are GLAD when we see them.

> *I remember when* God showed me that it is His Word that unites His people with each other and with Him.

Flight Of The Flu

It was a bad one. I had been in bed for two days, sleeping briefly, awaking only to find I was still sick. I longed to stay asleep until the thing would pass, but I was not able.

Being awake was a serious challenge. My stomach threatened constantly. There were aches and pains all over my body. Worse, I grew stiff in whatever position I lay. I just had to move, change my position, get relief.

Each time I'd awake the aches and pains would be somewhere else. I began to suspect that whatever muscles I used to change my position just before I dozed off were the exact ones that hurt the next time I awoke.

Moving was a very careful operation. A whole series of orders were in effect. "The stomach must be considered above all other things. Do not disturb the stomach. It is upset enough. It hasn't had food, it doesn't want food, it may never want food. Move gingerly. Don't stress those muscles." Ouch! Then I would lay there, waiting for sleep to return. And so it went, night and day.

Part way through the first day of these endless cycles, I decided to use my time awake to pray for Peter. He was a young man I knew who was locked in a battle with drugs. I had come to know his wife, children, niece, father, mother and grandfather. Often, one or more of them were passengers in my van as my family and I went to church. They all wanted God to give Peter a solution to his problem with heroin.

Peter wanted to be set free too. He wanted to get his family back together. He wasn't making it. Many people were praying for him, but there was no victory yet. As I lay there in misery, I decided to fill my waking minutes with prayer for Peter. Satan had me grounded but he hadn't shut off my mind. So, I started to pray and kept on praying.

Things were no better the second day. Morning, noon and afternoon had come and gone. Sleep, wake, ache, move, pray, sleep . . . It seemed it could go on for ever.

Evening came and I heard the family preparing for dinner in the next room. Their talk was subdued, quiet for my benefit no doubt.

By now, I was becoming practiced at praying for Peter. I had set my mind to it. Better than whining to myself about the flu. It was not so much a series of prayers as it was one ongoing petition, occasionally interrupted by a few minutes of sleep. Of course, all the prayer words were in my mind. I didn't dare open my mouth to speak out loud for fear of challenging my poor agonizing stomach.

My prayer must have reached some sort of crescendo now. I don't recall the words that were rumbling through my flu-fogged mind. What I do recall, what I shall always recall and never forget is this:

God spoke!

I Remember When . . .

I heard Him!

He spoke right out loud, right there in my bedroom. Even stranger, He spoke with the commanding, demanding, energizing power and intensity and curtness of a Marine Corps Drill Sergeant, something I hadn't heard in about 20 years. Loud too!

"If you're going to pray like that, you better get out of that bed and go eat dinner with your family!"

It was not the kind of command you ignore or question. Instantly, in one motion, I threw back the blankets, swung my feet to the floor, stood up straight, stretched a little, put my feet in my slippers, grabbed my bathrobe, and headed for the kitchen. As I went, I took inventory. My knees weren't wobbling. I couldn't sense any aches or pains. My stomach seemed docile, even hungry.

My wife and children stared in silent amazement as I passed by my empty place at the table, on my way to the cabinet for a plate and utensils. When they did speak, they were still whispering.

I ate. I was fine. I slept all night. I went to work the next day. My flu was gone. I had touched God and God had touched me.

Peter's victory came later.

I remember when God recognized my faith in prayer for someone else and counted it faith sufficient for my own needs.

A Focus On Eternity

Our daughter Valerie was 20 years old at the time. She had completed several years of college at Oral Roberts University in Oklahoma. During those years she participated in many school activities.

Valerie was always a good student. She made some very special friends at college. She had a sense of compassion for the needs of others that was unusual.

As in the years before, she was coming home to New York State for the Summer. Valerie was always full of life, vigor and excitement. Yet at this time she had a serious endeavor afoot, something that was the desire of her heart. Her goal was to draw as close to God as she possibly could.

On May 6, 1979 she wrote in her personal journal:

Dear Lord,

Please let your glory abide upon me.

Please send your Spirit to rest upon my head.

Surround me with the cloud of God,
So that the things of this world
Become dimmed to my eyes.

Make me acutely conscious of your presence.

Make me to know that there is <u>nothing</u> without you.

I Remember When . . .

Teach me to wait the "six days."

Teach me to value your Word above anything else,
> Anything I would be doing,
> The time I would be spending.

Call to me. Speak to me. I'm Listening.

This prayer is a reference to Exodus 24:15-17

> *And Moses went up into the mount, and a cloud covered the mount.*
>
> *And the glory of the LORD abode upon mount Sinai,*
>
> **and the cloud covered it six days: and the seventh day he called unto Moses out of the midst of the cloud.**
>
> *And the sight of the glory of the LORD was like devouring fire on the top of the mount in the eyes of the children of Israel.*

I remember when God showered joy on me by showing me the words of a beloved daughter lifting up the Word of God as the most important thing in her life.

Cathedral Park

For a certain number of years, I was blessed with a special place of retreat. I have always desired to be outdoors in the warmth of the sun, preferably near some body of water. River or lake, stream or ocean, even a little frog pond would do. However, it was my lot in life, most of the time, to work indoors, often in an office where the outside world could not be seen at all.

At this particular time, I had found a partial but welcome solution. Just a few minutes drive from my office was a small waterfront park. It was long and narrow, hemmed in between a high rock cliff and the Hudson River. There were trees and a walkway, picnic tables, and some spectacular vistas that allowed me to see down the river for miles.

In summer months, I spent as many noon times as possible at the park. The park would have just a few people in it. I could sit in the sun or sit in the shade as the day demanded, eat my lunch, watch the river, read the Word, meditate, pray, and praise God.

Even on days when the weather was less hospitable to my plans, I sometimes went to the park. Lunch was eaten in the car, but there was the same peace, the same withdrawal from the demands of the world, the same drawing into the presence of God. It was an easy place to praise God.

I found other times to go to the park. A few times I took a half day vacation there. There were times when I felt a special need for emotional relaxation or for focused prayer. Once I spent hours there, fruitlessly striving to memorize some scripture verses my Pastor had assigned. (I know that the truth and the understanding of the Word penetrated to my inner being, but I could develop no long term ability to repeat it, word for word, from memory. It just seemed to evaporate. Yet, the meaning, the significance, the importance never left me.)

On occasion, I would allow some trusted Christian friend to join me at the park. Usually these noon times were spent on spiritual reflections, or perhaps with spiritual counsel about not-to-spiritual problems. Sometimes we rehearsed plans for future ministry.

There were always things to see at the river. The long strings of railroad cars, arduously following their steel path, more that a mile away across the river; The Mid-Hudson bridge, small among suspension bridges but known far and wide for it's graceful beauty; large oil tankers and barges, moving upstream loaded with cargo and low in the water; the same vessels another day heading downstream empty, several yards higher; wild Japanese iris blooming in the gentle tidal wash of the river.

But mostly, there was tranquility. The bustling world was hushed. Even the sound of traffic on the nearby bridge was screened by the weeping willow trees. And always, there was the awesomeness of a cathedral, as God's presence permeated His creation.

Years later, long after it was no longer practical for me to visit the park, I hear a recording by Jim Reeves singing a song called My Cathedral.

Cathedral Park

My cathedral has a ceiling of blue.
My cathedral 'neath the sky,
Where I may lift up my eyes unto the hills,
And hear music from a stream rippling by.

My cathedral has an altar of flowers.
Their fragrant incense fills the air.
In my cathedral I am closer to Him
Than I could be anywhere.

For here I pray in a place so grand.
The carpet I kneel on was made by His own hand.
My cathedral has candles lighted by the stars
And mighty pillars of trees.

No other cathedral is so beautiful,
For God made my cathedral for me.

I remember when, for a season, for a few special years, the park was my cathedral. There I could meet with Him and resolve the needs of the day.

Trusting

Sometimes what you know is true, but it is not enough. You need to know more.

It can be that way when we select a scripture to meet the need before us. The implication is that one scripture, one truth, can do it all. Pick the one that fits the best, or the one you like the best, or the one you know the best, and hope for the best. Of course, that's not what God intended when He gave us His Word.

While there are probably not many who would do this on purpose, many might do it by accident. We might do it because of a lack of a full knowledge of scripture. We might do it because, even though we have that knowledge, we have overlooked a relevant verse. If we are to walk in the fullness of the scripture, we need to purposefully seek out all the pieces that fit our situation. We must not be content with the one verse that comes to our mind or the one that our friend provides or the one verse which an exhorter brings before us. We need to go back to the whole word and find the wholeness of the word.

This was driven home to me with much force on an occasion when I fully believed I was doing the right thing. It was many years ago. I was employed by a major American company. The department to which I belonged consisted of about fifteen people with offices in three different cities. As I left my office on a Friday afternoon, although I didn't realize it, things were about to change.

When I arrived for work the following Monday morning, I discovered that what had been a department of fifteen, existing at three locations, was now a department of three existing at one location. I was not one of the three.

Well, not to fear. After all, the Company had a history of never laying anyone off. It was part of a growth industry. They always hired, never fired. I knew an assignment would be along promptly. That was the way of the business. And on the spiritual side, I had great faith that God would provide. After all, He was my source, not the Company. Did not the scripture say that He knows my needs even before I ask. All I needed to do was continue to worship Him, trust Him, walk my life, and await the solution. "God will take care of me."

Many Christians would accept that position. Many would even actively and assertively teach that position. Indeed, it is a valid position, as far as it goes. But the Lord was about to give me personal instruction in the shortcomings and narrowness of this view.

For a few weeks there was really no problem. I went to my office each day. I did some reading. I cleaned up some odds and ends. I reorganized my belongings. I caught up on some outside errands.

Of course, I received my regular pay check. That was the Company way. Respect for the individual, a basic Company tenet was in operation. There was no stress, no challenge, just a wait.

But then time began to drag. To show up in the same old office at the same old desk, with really nothing to do, got to be a bit boring. I enrolled in some internal education courses that were available. I studied new Company products that were becoming available. I wanted to make use of the time. But weeks went by. Months went by. At last, a whole quarter of a year had passed, twelve whole weeks!

Although there was no economic pressure and no management pressure, there was now a psychological pressure growing in me. Twelve weeks! I developed a sense of being unattached. I was without a peer group. I was on the shelf. I was worth nothing to the company. I was more of a problem than a resource, an expense instead of a profit. Dismay began to set in. Day by day these feelings grew. More and more, I dreaded going to the office in the morning. This was indeed an odd and new kind of pain for me.

Finally, I'd had enough. About seven o'clock on a workday morning, I kneeled on the den carpet in front of my old oak rocker. It was a place where the Lord and I met frequently. This day I spoke to Him earnestly. I do not remember my exact words. I'm sure they were not eloquent. I do remember the earnestness of my petition. The sense of my prayer was, "God, give me a solution to this! I want out of this situation! I don't know how, but get me out." Then I went off to the empty desk in the empty office.

Unknown to me, later that very same morning, at about 11 o'clock, some managers were meeting.

They decided to create a new position. At one o'clock, when I returned from lunch, I was invited into a manager's office. The new position was offered to me. I was astounded! Not only was there an opportunity, there was a wonderfully good fit for my experience and my skills. I would be working for a man I respected as a manager. I would be productive again. I would even be able to use some of the information I had gained in those recent courses. The trial was over.

As I went away rejoicing about God's provision, my heart and mind turned to him and in essence I said, "How come?" Wrapped up in that question was a whole set of little questions like, "What took so long?" and "Why now?" The Holy Spirit spoke to me instantly: *"You had not because you asked not."* And I responded, "But I trusted, I trusted . . . I trusted, I expected, . . . I trusted!" Then the Holy Spirit spoke again, *"It is good that you trusted, but you must also ask."*

When you ask, God is quick to answer. I had trusted for 12 weeks. He answered within 6 hours. I had asked at 7am. He created at 11am. That put a new meaning to the phrase, 7-11.

And so,

I learned that scripture is not to be selected. It is to be added.

I learned that when we face a situation wherein we need the truth of the Word, we should not be satisfied with the first truth we discern.

I learned that we must seek further truth, additional truth, that we might know the full truth.

Also, because of this experience I became even more quick to discern the error of those who teach from a single passage without recourse to the remainder of the Word; those who have found it convenient to seize upon a single theme without considering the other truths that relate to it. For you see, a second truth does not negate the first truth. A third truth does not negate the first and the second. Rather, they add to each other bringing clarity, completeness and wondrous insight and wisdom.

Had I been punished? No!

Had I been instructed? Yes.

Had I been blessed? Indeed!

I had been loved and comforted for my trusting and I had been taught to ask as well. I had trusted for three months, but never asked.

How long might I have waited if I asked at the beginning but never trusted? Can one ask without trusting? Yes, they can. They often do. They wait and wait and wait, until trust rises up within them. Yes, we must do both –Trust and Ask.

> *I remember when God, in a most dramatic way, taught me a personal lesson about believing and asking.*

A Day At The Lake

I was more or less talking to myself.

"Three days ago we closed the annual week-long anniversary celebration of the church. There were special speakers and special manifestations of the Holy Spirit. It was strenuous and wearing, but God had moved in marvelous life-changing ways."

"Yesterday was the home-going celebration for Ray, a young father in our church who had come to love God."

"Tomorrow I have five appointments for counsel, guidance, planning. Strange fare for a Business Administrator, but that is what God is doing."

"Today is mine."

These were my reflections that Tuesday morning in September. I wanted some time away from the churning, bubbling days; time to refresh; time to lock out the rumble of life; time to draw into God's peaceful presence.

I was at Candlewood Lake. I was alone with my boat and my notebooks. Perhaps it would be a time to write in this book. During the weeks of Summer, I had been here several times. In turn, I had brought my wife Helen, my daughter Laura, my son Larry, and Pastor to the lake. Now the seasons were about to turn. My opportunities were running out. Today I was here alone, alone with Jesus.

I Remember When . . .

The lake was quiet that morning, a few days after Labor Day. Kids were back in school. The parking lot at the ramp had only two cars and one boat trailer when I arrived about 10 a.m., instead of the many that usually crowd it.

For the first hour on the lake, I cruised slowly, as slowly as I could make the boat go. It makes little noise at that speed. The sky was a brilliant blue with a few bright white clouds. In every direction were green hills, preparing to change color in just a few weeks. The temperature was perfect, the warmth of the sun pleasant on my back. In this utopia of peace I cruised along, standing behind the wheel, slowly relaxing the tensions that had built up, praising God, singing aloud in my Heavenly language.

As time passed, words began to occasionally infiltrate, English words. They were some part of a song I hadn't heard in years. I was reluctant to let them interfere with my spiritual praise. For a while I consciously fought them off. Then, as they continued to press my mind, I couldn't suppress them any more. I began to sing --

> *"Come to the water.*
> *Stand by my side.*
> *I know you are thirsty.*
> *You won't be denied."*

Then back to tongues again. The song came again. Then back to tongues. The 4th or 5th time this happened, I suddenly understood something:

"This is not just an old song creeping out from the recesses of my mind."

"This is not an ordinary song that Christians sing to praise God."

"This is a special song."

"God is singing this song!"

"These words are from Him."
"He is singing it to me!"
"Here! Now! Today!"
"I am not being interrupted."
"I am being answered!"

"Come to the water. Stand by my side."

Yes, come to the living water. But also, I had come to the lake water to "stand by His side," to be with Him.

"I know you are thirsty."

Yes Lord . . .

"You won't be denied."

Praise you Jesus!

Yes, the day was for me. Then, for the next three hours I sat on my favorite rock at the side of the lake, in the mottled shade of a big oak tree, and I wrote in this book. The Holy Spirit poured forth insights and reminiscences at a rapid pace, and I scribbled as I raced to keep up. Times and pages flew by.

Then I took a break. I went for a swim. Refreshing. Pleasant. When I came out of the water, I walked back to the rock. I just stood there for a while, drying in the sun, absorbing the beauty that surrounded me, being thankful for this time of peace and tranquility.

The rock, my favorite rock, is an interesting one. It is not a boulder, but a large outcropping of solid rock, reaching down into the water of the lake. It has lines in it, more or less parallel lines. Black, Gray, White. Black, Gray, White. It is interesting to the eye to see all these patterns and colors; Especially the part that is wet. The wet part has so much more -- life. I was so impressed by that view. I said to God, "Lord, I don't know how it was made but I know who it was made by. It's so beautiful."

This rock is interesting when it's dry, but it's beautiful when it's wet.

So many times I have picked up pebbles and shells at the sea shore because of their brilliant colors and patterns, only to be disappointed by their dullness when they became dry and lost their glistening sheen. I have even put some in bottles with water so I could again see their brilliant patterns of color and shade.

I stood there looking at the rock, looking at the contrast between the wet part and the dry part. "Lord, is there a spiritual parallel to this?"

Then at once, instantly, I knew that there is a parallel. It is this:

We humans are as the rocks and pebbles and shells.

A Day At The Lake

We are God's creation, filled with the glory and beauty of His design.

But we project that glory dully, unless we are washed with water, the water of the Word.

The washing with the water of the Word makes us glisten and glow and show the beauty that is buried within us.

But when the wave of washing has passed, and the heat of the day, the turmoil of life, has evaporated its deposit, we, like the rock, turn dry and dull again.

Then, His glory is not seen in us.

For His glory to radiate from us, we must be washed in His Word constantly.

I had come to this place dry. Now I was wet.

And so, back to writing in this book.

Later, as the boat roared toward the loading ramp and home, I was praising God again. I was rejoicing. My mind was overwhelmed. I had begun the day by singing to Him, and He came and sang to me.

I couldn't contain myself. My whole being wanted to praise Him. Spontaneously, I shouted out in joy! "Praise You Lord!" He had given me my time of peace and refreshment and illumination. What personal communion we had shared!

Amazed, excited, elevated, I shouted again, louder this time, full of joy and marvel:

"Lord, you knock my socks off ! ! !"

. . . Then I glanced down at the floor of the boat, at my bare feet, and I realized how appropriate my exclamation had been,

and I laughed and laughed and laughed and laughed.

Oh, we had a wonderful time that day, God and I, alone together on our lake.

I remember when I went out weary and God not only met me but He refreshed me, He instructed me and He lifted up my heart in joy.

Ol' Blue

The jacket didn't look old, even though it was far from new. It was a blazer, dark blue, almost navy. It had, in fact, been around for years. However, the synthetic thread of which the cloth was woven had held up well. Many wearings over many years had taken no evident toll.

The week before this occasion, I had worn it to church on Sunday morning. Gray slacks, a white shirt and a dark blue tie had completed the outfit. Casual compared to a suit, dressed up compared to a crew neck shirt and Jeans, you might call it a typical ushers' uniform. Well, not really. Usually an ushers' uniform would have a brighter tie, probably a medium dark red with a print of some sort. Not me, not usually anyway. I owned patterned red ties that I wore at other times, but with this jacket I really liked that solid dark blue tie. And, since I wasn't an usher anyway, I could make my own choices.

That was all last week. This week, as I dressed on Sunday morning, I stared at my wardrobe. It isn't huge, but it is comfortable enough to provide some interesting variety. I had several choices, each of which would be both comfortable and appropriate, but . . . I wanted to wear the dark blue jacket again! Then the conversation began between "me" and "myself." ("I" didn't get involved.)

"You wore that last Sunday," me said to myself. "Yes," myself responded, "but no one will notice. No one has ever noticed this jacket in the dozens and dozens of times it's been to church. They notice the suede jacket and the brown suit, but never this one."

"Me" being easily convinced, the matter was quickly settled. Ol' Blue was going to church again. Just to satisfy the misgivings of wearing the same thing two Sundays in a row, "I" chose a different tie: dark red with a pattern of small blue and gold ovals. Now "me," "myself," and "I" were all satisfied.

As usual, I arrived at church early. The heat needed to be adjusted throughout the building. Air flow patterns had to be set up. The choir and the band were already gathering to practice for the morning worship service. My tasks accomplished, I retired to my office for the regular Sunday morning breakfast I had brought of Danish and coffee.

Almost at once, Skip came energetically walking up the corridor that passed by my office door. Seeing me at my desk, he abruptly changed his course and swerved into the room. He greeted me cordially and immediately began to rejoice in what God had been doing in his life. Skip was just overflowing with enthusiasm for his Lord and the new life He had given him in recent months. Then, suddenly, the topic changed: "That's a nice jacket you've got on. I like that. It's not too dark. Just seeing it makes me feel awake." Then he was gone, scooting down the hall to bless someone else.

As he departed, I thought, "Well, Skip is a nice friendly guy. It's great to have friends around – it's just a plain old coat."

Ten minutes later I was returning from a check of the building. I ran into Dave at a corner where two hallways merged. He fell into step just to the right and about a foot behind me. "Hey, I like your jacket Brother Al. That's real sharp!" The words were spoken before I had fully realized that it was Dave who had come up upon me. "Uh, thanks," I spouted in my surprise.

Later, as I stood in the service, praising God in the midst of the congregation, immersed in the power of His presence that can be felt so strongly at such times, I reflected on those two comments. An old jacket, an outfit so standard that it could be given a number, such as usher-3, an absolutely transparent jacket that no one had ever seen or noticed for years, and TWO compliments in this ONE morning!

"What does it mean Lord? How come? Maybe it was the red tie? What else could it be?"

Late that evening, as I puzzled over the matter again, the answer became obvious. In His own way of speaking to my understanding, God gave the answer. Here are my words to describe the understanding God gave me:

"Skip and Dave love Me. Long before they arrived at church they had clothed themselves in My presence and in My Love. Their excitement and joy at being in the company of their brothers and sisters was so full that they couldn't help but let some of that love spurt out and become words. They love you Al, because you are mine, along with them. They love us so much, you and Me, that even your old blue jacket looks new to them. They are seeing with My eyes. You are all new creatures together."

Yes, I am loved. Skip and Dave love me. Many others do too. They are glad when their eyes fall on me, for I too have trusted in His Word. (Psalm 119:74**)**

I remember when God used my old blue jacket to reveal the love of my brothers in Christ.

Rejoicing Together

For a certain number of years I owned a one-man travel van that I called Blue Haven. I had built it up myself to meet my needs and wishes. I used it to satisfy my desire to see some of the majestic sites in this nation. There were trips to the National Parks of the west, to Lake Powell, to New Orleans and the delta, and many other places.

I also used it to shorten my exposure to the winter months in New York State. A two or three week vacation to South Carolina shores in the middle of November helped accomplish that at the start of the winter season. A trip to favorite Florida sites in March did likewise when Spring was around the corner. This continued for several years as I accumulated over nine months of overnight stays in my well equipped van.

Most of these trips were alone, because piano students and flower beds took priority over travel opportunities as far as my wife was concerned. So, we talked and agreed and I went.

In those days when I was traveling alone, I sometimes stopped to visit friends who had moved away from the old New York area where we remained. Sometimes I even stayed overnight.

It was on one of these visits that I was asked what could be called a very provocative question. It was personal, almost impolite. Now, this was a couple I was visiting. I had a close personal relationship with each of them. We had known each other for years.

71

I loved them and they loved me. They didn't ask the question out of anything other than concern for my well being.

> "We've been talking and we're concerned about you. You travel to all these beautiful places and see all these wonderful things. But you are alone. You have no one to share them with. How can you handle that? Doesn't it make you feel awfully lonely?"

I had not anticipated the question. There were no conversational clues leading up to it. I was startled by how personal a question it was. Then, quickly, I realized that it was born of concern for me and my well being. These were my friends who cared for me. I owed them the best answer I could give.

It is a continuing blessing that I had a ready answer to this unanticipated question.

I began by recalling that at one time, at the beginning, I did have some of those thoughts. As a matter of fact, I had the exact sense of loneliness they had described. Then one day, insight arrived and companionship blossomed.

The only reason I was lonely was that I felt I had no one there with whom to share the beautiful and interesting things I saw. That was the only pain -- No one there to share with.

But when I looked at others nearby, I realized the expectation was false. None of them had someone to fully share with even though they were in couples or groups. The cares of the world, real and imagined, often obliterated the pleasure.

Distraction, weariness, different interests diluted the sharing.

Being alone was actually fuller, and more focused.

My insight was not the result of a formal prayer. It came in response to an earnest heartfelt question. Then, I set my mind to make God my partner. He is the Creator of the marvels I see. Instead of wanting to say to someone, "Look at the colors in that sunset!" I determined in my heart to say, "Thank you Lord, that's beautiful, you're so generous...!"

He is right there, present at every glory. He is more delighted in the things I see than even I am. They are His creation. He called them "Good."

How could I be lonely when the God of the universe is sharing His loved creation with me.

He's never tired, cranky or absent. As a matter of fact,

When I experience delight
in seeing His creations
It is because He made me in His image and
I am seeing them with His eyes.

Years later I heard a portion of a song, sung by John Starns, that sums it up well:

73

" I didn't ask for riches,
But you gave me wealth untold,
The moon and the stars, the sun in the sky,
    And He gave me eyes to behold."

"I thank the Lord for everything
And I count all my blessings each day,
For He came to me when I needed Him,
    I only had to pray."

I remember when God helped me to understand that the beauty I behold is beautiful to me because it is beautiful to Him.

Cherry Strudel

It was a quiet sunny morning – time for a relaxing breakfast before the start of a busy day. I sat at the table with my fresh brewed coffee and a slice of an excellent cherry strudel. As baked goods go, I am a bit partial to things with a cherry fruit filling: cherry pies, cherry turnovers, cherry strudel. And this strudel was not only cherry, but it had an excellent blend of flavor and texture, not too tart, not too sweet. In short, it was a delight. Ummm.

As I sipped my coffee and ate my slice of prime strudel, I read the morning paper. This was not an unusual way for me to start the day. After all, one has to catch up on the local news sometime. The mind is not really needed to drink coffee and eat strudel. Why not put it to use on some of the other needs of the day?

About half way through the strudel process, I became freshly alert to a fact of life:

One cannot enjoy anything
without paying attention to it!

The strudel was half gone, my pleasant strudel, and I had not "tasted" it. Except for the fact that it had started to cool, the coffee would have escaped my attention too. There I was, mechanically eating my savory treat and paying it no respect whatsoever! It might bring me nourishment but it was bringing me no sensory pleasure. My focus was on the newspaper. My mind was on the newspaper. My being was absorbed by the newspaper. I was oblivious to the good things around me. My eating had become mechanical, a bit like walking to the mailbox: mind on the mail, feet walking by themselves. Here I was, mind on the newspaper, mouth eating by itself.

Now, this seemed like a real waste of a Good Cherry Strudel. I determined to pay attention to the flavors in my mouth and enjoy them and relate to them. They would soon be gone. And I did. I ignored the paper and closed my eyes and focused my mind on the taste and texture of the strudel. Ummm! Somehow, closed eyes seem to help focus the mind.

Then, as I savored my cherry strudel, I began to thank God again for the bounty I was enjoying. This was a step more than the "Grace" I had already "said." This was a mentally verbalized appreciation for the care and the presence of my God, my Creator, my Supplier, my Sustainer. Cherry strudel is not too small a thing to thank God for. I even thanked Him for reminding me to pay attention to it and to actually savor it. It had been a blessing, present but unnoticed. Yes, a blessing, present, but not savored. How wasteful. How foolish.

Suddenly I remembered another fact of life:

> *It's not just cherry strudel that is present*
> *but not savored.*

It is God Himself.

There He is, with me, every moment of my life, blessing me, available to be savored for His great goodness, but my mind is often oblivious to Him. I consume the blessings of His presence without even noticing their delightfulness. I take and use the gifts without sufficient notice of the Giver. If I have daily devotions and prayer time, that is nice and good. To have constant, attentive communion is so much better.

It is all a matter of interruptions.

It can be like this:

- My communion with my God can be an interruption in the flow of the activities found in my daily life.
- I can spend hours and hours of each day with never a glance toward Him.
- Sometimes the activities of the day can threaten even that small space of time I had reserved to be with Him.
- My daily life flow can endure only a small interruption to pay attention to my Heavenly Father.

Or, it can be like this:

- The activities of my daily life can be an interruption in the flow of my communion with God.
- I can make Him a constant presence in my mind.
- I can joyfully thank Him for each blessing as it is revealed.
- I can recruit His wisdom for every activity of my day.
- I can fill the nooks and crannies of my time with praise.

- I can momentarily excuse myself, apply the skills He has given me to deliver to the world, then hastily return to Him.

It may seem rude to suggest that one interrupt God. It is not. To interrupt God one must be in His presence. That is far more joy to Him than an occasional "Hello!" from a distant heart.

Remember –

One cannot <u>enjoy</u> anything without paying <u>attention</u> to it!

Close your eyes if you must.
Let the world be dimmed.
Be sure to savor the Gift.
Honor God!

One of the mottos of Blessed Man Ministries is -

*Honoring the God of gifts
Rejoicing in the gifts of God*

I remember when God called my attention to His constant presence and my opportunity to fellowship with Him, all day, every day.

Gifts From The Sea

A Bit Of Background

Have you been to the ocean beach? If you have
ever spent some time there, you know it can be very
active and dynamic. Sometimes it is even noisy and
threatening. Huge waves roar in from the open
ocean and crash on the sandy shore. With their
great power, they drag in and toss up all kinds of
things: sea shells, shell fragments, colorful stones,
sea weed, pieces of wood. Sometimes they even
rearrange the shape of the sandy beach. Then, if
you walk along the beach a day or so later, after the
ocean has calmed down, you might find some really
interesting things to pick up and take home and
display.

There are other times when the ocean is calm and
serene. Little waves rise and fall, inviting you to
come into the water and rock back and forth with
them. Since they are small, without much power,
they carry in nothing. There are no gifts from a calm
sea.

Even so, I like the calm times. It is then that the
gentle surf seems able to drive away the "noise" of
everyday life. It is as if the gentle wash of the surf
on the sand was washing way the cares of the world
from my mind. Yes, I have always found something
especially peaceful about the calm ocean beach.

I like to walk along the sand, ankle deep in the surf,
feeling the glow of the sun and the brush of the
breeze. It seems relaxing and pleasant. In those

79

times I like to focus my mind on God and His Word. After all, He created this wonderful place. Why not say thank-you to Him as I enjoy it?

Through the years, I have sought out places and times for exactly such re-creation. God and I, together at the seashore, have shared some wonderful times. Three of these were really unusual.

Earlier Days

When I walk the sea shore, my eyes are mostly on the surf line. I am always looking for a prize, a gift from the sea. The surf line is where you are most likely to see freshly arrived sea shells. Sometimes, even though the last storm was weeks ago, you might find something special that no one else has found yet.

I really like looking at sea shells. There are so many kinds, colors and shapes. I especially like conch shells and their cousins, the various forms of whelks. The good news is that whelks can sometimes be found in my part of the world. They have always been wonderful to me: the spirals, the spikes, the lines of color, the textures. To me they represent the epitome of exoskeletal extravagance. They're pretty too!

When I was a youngster, Mom had a lovely Queen Conch on display in her china cabinet. It was a special token to her, purchased on some long ago occasion, well before my days. (Mom never got to spend time at the shore searching for her own "find.")

My wife, Helen, liked shells too. We have several special samples in our home. They came from far parts of the world. We bought them during our various excursions to the sea. Each is unique in color, form and visual impact.

It is nice to be able to buy a shell someone else has found, but what an exciting thing it must be to discover one of these gems of the sea yourself! What a delight to rescue it from it's hiding place in the deep and put it on display in your own home or office!

For many years the family strolled the edge of the sea at vacation time. We always stared at the surf line, hoping to discover some especially fine shell specimen. All that ever came our way of conch shells were battered fragments. You could walk for days without finding a whole, well preserved whelk shell. Clams, oysters, scallops, snails and who knows what other varieties all donated themselves to our amusement. They wound up making a new home in our jars and baskets. Many had beautiful shadings of color, even more so when wet. Scallop shells were always plentiful along the shore of Cape Cod Bay. You could have a collection of hundreds of them alone, and still have no two with exactly the same markings. Beautiful to see and fun to find. Thank you Lord.

Years after the family times, I had converted my van into a mini-RV, named it Blue Haven, and was making an occasional trip to the ocean. On one such trip, I became captivated by a particular shell I found sliding along in the surf. It was a whelk shell that had seen better days. It had been sliding back and forth in the surf, rubbing against the abrading sand, for so long that one side had quite worn away. Yet the parts that remained still held some interesting patterns of color and shape. As I examined it, I was struck by a thought: I was holding in my hand the life residue of a creature that had come to life in the sea, grown and prospered in the sea, received it's necessary nourishment from the sea; it was a sea-being and now it's days had passed.

In a way, I was a sea-being also. The sea was important to me. The sea hadn't birthed me and grown me and prospered me, but I always felt we belonged to each other, the sea and I.

I saved that well-worn shell and later mounted it in a frame and hung it in my office. The idea was to help me remember the sea and it's pleasantness during times of stress and strain.

It was also to remind me that life is fleeting and I should be sure to visit my sea often, to use every opportunity. My buddy on the wall had used up all his opportunities, but I still had some. Yes, I should seek out opportunities to enjoy the blessings God has provided.

> *I remember when God used a worn and battered sea shell to focus my mind on the temporary nature of life and to recognize that the opportunities of life are limited.*

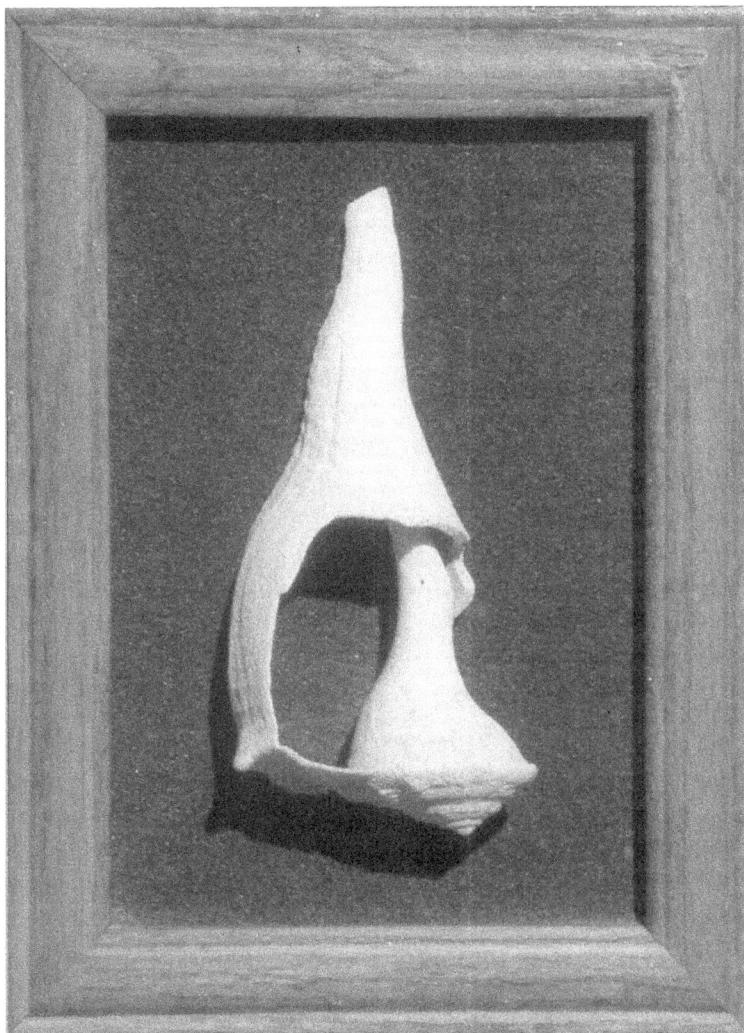

An Amazing Encounter

Not everything God does comes with crashing thunder or flashing lights. Sometimes He uses the gentle murmur of the seaside surf or the ripples of a flowing current. Most wonderful of all is that He delights in bringing delight to His children. He loves us and wants to make us happy.

Blue Haven and I were at the Apache campground at Myrtle Beach, South Carolina. It was November and I was on one of my "delay winter as much as you can" trips. The idea was to enjoy the still-warm south while the winter began to bluster in New York. I had chosen Myrtle Beach as an acceptable trade-off between warmth and travel distance.

Blue Haven was parked no more than 30 feet from the high tide line. The pleasant murmur of the surf was in my ears as I fell asleep and as I awoke. It said "good night" and it said "good morning." The November nights were cool, but the days were delightful: sunny, warm and pleasant.

Much of the "sand" at this stretch of ocean beach was not sand at all. It was finely ground sea shells. A piece one inch across was rare. Whole shells, even small ones, were completely absent. Nonetheless, it was fun to walk in the surf. The sunshine was comfortable and the ocean offered a free dunking to cool me off whenever I wanted it to. So, my days there passed at a leisurely pace as I walked, first north for a couple miles, then back to Blue Haven for lunch, then south for another mile or so and back.

84

An Amazing Encounter

I had arrived at Myrtle Beach late on a Saturday afternoon and settled in. My departure from my office at the Center had been hectic. Although the trip had been planned and scheduled months in advance, last minute needs made me feel as if I was fleeing a burning building. The biggest impact was to my self-confidence: What have I forgotten to take, to do, to provide for???

Finally it was time to leave. As I strode through the open door of my office, briefcase in my left hand, keys in my right, I flicked off the lights and stepped out into the corridor, pulling the door behind me. Inside myself, I was in a mild panic about the "forgottens."

Just before the door latched shut, I stopped it. I had remembered something. I flipped the lights back on and darted back in to grab "The Tape." "The Tape" had been in my office for over a year, but I never found time to listen to it. It was a message by one of my favorite preachers. I had no idea what it was about, but maybe, while I was away, I would finally find time to hear it. Maybe there was something on it that was important for me to know. "The Tape" in hand, I hastily made my escape.

I was at Myrtle Beach several days before I was really relaxed and at ease. It was now Thursday, November 18th, 1993. The tension had slowly drained away and my blood pressure was at peace. In the early afternoon I trotted away from Blue Haven, heading for the surf and my energetic walk to what I called the south inlet. Yesterday I had seen a great blue heron there, watching the surf for his lunch. What a stately image. Maybe he would be there today too and I could see him again.

I hadn't gone far along the surf line when it came. Was it just a notion or a nudge from the Holy Spirit? The thought was to return to Blue Haven and get my Walkman and listen to "The Tape" as I walked to the inlet. "No! I've already started. I'm not going back," I thought.

Again it came, "The Tape." Again, "No! I know it's not far, but no."

Once more, "The Tape!" The third summons and the sense of demand that came with it were powerful. This time I yielded. Instantly, I executed a good old Marine Corps "to the rear" marching movement. I pivoted 180 degrees on the ball of my foot and set out in the opposite direction, without even slowing down.

Then it happened. That first step after pivoting was one of the most remarkable steps of my life. As my foot hit the sand on my first stride back, the surf washed an intact Knobbed Whelk shell right across it. It rolled right across my foot! I stumbled a bit trying to stop my motion. I grabbed at the shell before the waves could wash it away.

It was nearly six inches long, beautifully colored and only slightly sea-worn. A gift for me! A gift from the sea! A gift from God, bestowed because of my obedience. Did God create that shell at that very instant? I don't know. I don't think so. But I do know that it blessed me. I also know that I would never have seen it if I didn't obey and reverse my direction at the exact moment I did. Over the years there were many more days at Myrtle Beach, but there never was another whole shell. Not even a whole clam shell.

So I took the shell, my shell, and returned to Blue Haven. After a little time spent studying the intricate shapes and color patterns of my new gift, I left again for my ocean walk. My Walkman and The Tape went with me. I never saw the great blue heron again, but I had a wonderful day. The Tape? It was a blessing and a timely instruction to me, but that is a story for another time.

The Shell From Myrtle Beach

I remember when God taught me that heeding the urgings of the Holy Spirit can lead to instant rewards.

Words In Season

The trip had been wonderful. Blue Haven and I had been on the road for nearly the whole month of June. I had once again visited some of my favorite scenic places of the West.

At Zion National Park I once again hiked the flowing steam of the Virgin River, amazed by the vertical walls of rock and the vistas hidden around each bend in the canyon.

At Lake Powell, I had the use of a small boat for a whole week, searching in and out of narrow flooded side canyons, filled with surprise vistas and awesome views.

I stood at an overlook at the north rim of the Grand Canyon and strained to take in the vastness and the beauty.

I saw many scenes and walked some miles of pathways, always engulfed in the beauty and glory of God's creation. We had a wonderful time together, He and I, rejoicing in His handiwork.

Then came the long trip home to New York. Frequent phone calls had kept me informed and I knew things were all well there. Being home again would soon bring a return to old patterns and familiar ways, the love of family and friends.

I had been so blessed and satisfied on this month long tour. It was a long time dream come true. It was a different thing than my regular "escape winter" trips, though that goal was still part of my inner desire.

Now I had one more day of travel before reaching home. I was in the state of Virginia and towards dusk I checked into a roadside campground for the night. Tomorrow I would be home, and the long planned tour that had blessed me so fully would be only a memory.

I slept soundly that night. Blue Haven was my comfortable abode. Early in the morning, about 7:30 or so, something strange happened. In the quiet dim dawn of the campground, in the secure privacy of Blue Haven, I was awakened by a male voice! I was instantly startled into full consciousness. Then I realized, it was MY voice. It was speaking in the morning dimness, out loud, not by my intent or direction. Even more dramatic was what I was saying:

"I am blessed going out and I am blessed coming in."

I objected. It is hard to argue with your own voice, but that is what my mind was doing. I had not approved this message! Beyond doubt, I had been blessed going out, but it was over, I was almost home. Going in was not part of the blessing! Going home was great and wonderful but the blessing was in going out. So my unruly mind opined – with vigor.

Nonetheless, the occurrence was so unusual that I made written note of it as soon as I was out of that bed. And I pondered, what does this mean? Of course I was familiar with Psalm 121 and the promise that God would keep us in our going out and our coming in. But this was different. This was me, my voice, spontaneously proclaiming in the still of the morning that I was not only blessed in the going out but also blessed in the coming in! Praise God from Whom all blessings flow.

I finished the trip home that day. Everything was great. Routines resumed. The year progressed. Some things changed in my environment. Many were subtle, some more dramatic. I didn't cause any of them. I just walked through doors that opened. When July came around again, a year later, those doorways that opened had led to a new and unanticipated blessing.

My wife and I had become full time residents of Florida. Good bye snows of New York. The "blessing coming in" had come to pass.

No amount of reasoning could have allowed me to anticipate what this blessing would be. It was only in retrospect that I saw and understood that I had been given a gift of promise that in time showed up as a gift of fact.

I remember when *God alerted me to the blessings He had in store for me, speaking to me of the future as I was focused on the past.*

A Rushing Stream

It was a Tuesday morning, April 27, 1999. I was
walking the beach again, this time at Vilano, the
southern tip of the island north of ours, here in
Florida. There is an inlet between the islands. It
connects the ocean with the intracoastal waterway.
Four times a day, a huge flow of water churns
through the inlet as the tide first fills, then empties
the waterway and the miles of marsh beyond. To
the south, the next inlet is about 20 miles away. The
next inlet to the north is more than 40 miles away.
So the flow through my inlet, St. Augustine inlet, is
indeed huge. While the intracoastal waterway in
Florida has a typical depth of 13 to 20 feet, the
center channel of the inlet has been gouged to a
depth of 47 feet by the fast flowing tide.

Dolphins are known to frequent this channel. I've
seen them many times. I imagine they are attracted
by the large schools of fish that sometimes ride in or
out on the tide. The old timers in the area call this
place Porpoise Point.

On this particular day I was walking on the pure fine
sand that edges the north side of the inlet. The
water was only up to my ankles as it streamed by,
but six feet away at the edge of the sandy shelf on
which I walked, I could see the tidal torrent tumbling
by, rushing into the bay.

I was in a melancholy mood that morning. Nothing
was really wrong in my life, but somehow it seemed
that things weren't right either. I just had this

ill-defined, down in the dumps, alone in the world feeling. I was at Porpoise Point because it was deserted and I knew that the natural cure for my ailment was the sand and the sea, the birds and the breeze, the sun and the surf. The charm of God's creation was wonderfully refreshing and praise was bubbling up within me as I thanked Him for it.

As I strolled along, slowly converting the beauty of my surroundings into energy for my soul, I began to think about other ocean times. Cape Cod. Florida Keys. Bonita Bay. Myrtle Beach.

Myrtle Beach! The whelk shell gift at Myrtle Beach! Oh, Wow! What a memory! Suddenly, I spoke right out loud,

"Lord, do you still do things like that?"

At that instant, at that very moment, I saw a whelk shell come rolling across that sandy shallow bottom, directly toward me. It stopped no more than 20 inches away from my toes and lay there. I knew my question had been answered.

When I picked up the shell I saw it was about the same size as the Myrtle Beach shell, but a little more sea-worn. As far as I was concerned, it could have been broken and colorless and ugly. It wouldn't have mattered. It was not the beauty of the shell that was filling me with excitement. No, I was filled with the joy of experiencing the timely personal attentions of my loving God. He had again given me a gift shell in a place where there could be no shells.

The Shell From Porpoise Point

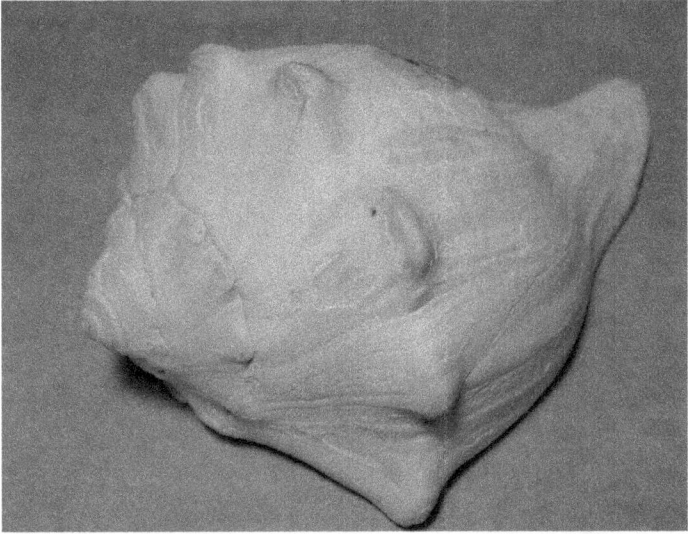

I remember when God showed me that however I feel, wherever I am, He is there to comfort me.

Strolling Onward

Years passed. It was now 2008. Blue Haven had been gone for more than 10 years. Travel had not been a part of my picture all that time. Such a long time. Many Blue Haven trips had been to Florida, and now I lived there. No need to travel there. But wait!

What about all those Florida State Parks I had once planned to visit. And there were friends in other states whom I hadn't seen in a long time. And a few places I would like to visit again and even some I had never visited. It wasn't all about Florida.

So, at the end of March I embarked on a new project: build a new one-man travel machine. I bought a used Toyota van and three weeks later I was ready to roll. Now this was not a replica of Blue Haven. The new van, Green Haven, was a civilized vehicle for carrying people, with seats and windows and all. I wanted to preserve it as much as possible. So, my design called for all the travel equipment to be removable, and not affect the internal structure of the van at all. At the end of three weeks, I had a bed, refrigerator, microwave, toaster oven, folding table, water supply, mini-sink, 1500 watts of on-board AC power, and storage space for food and clothes. Neat!

It was time for a test run. I choose to not go away overnight for the first excursion. Instead, I went to a nearby beach that I liked to visit, a place called Matanzas. I arrived a little after 8 AM, had breakfast, walked, read, walked some more, etc. Everything worked well and I was happy.

About 11 AM, I finished off my second cup of coffee, hopped out of the van, and strolled to the edge of the water. As I stood there in the bright sun with the waves gently breaking around my ankles, I remembered other ocean times. I was happy as I thought of the whelk shell that God delivered right to my foot at Ocean Grove. I thought of the other whelk shell at Vilano Beach at the edge of the St. Augustine inlet. I am sure there was a bit of a grin on my face as words came to my mind. These words were not spoken out loud. I felt foolish to even think them, let alone say them. Yet, my mind spoke,

 "Wouldn't it be something if I found a whelk shell right here, right now? On this first day out with Green Haven? Like those other times?"

Then I thought,

"Anything can happen, I better look down at the surf instead of out to sea."

" What's that rolling over there?"

"Oh my!"

One step away from where I stood in the surf, a whelk shell rolled up. I saw it coming toward me. I grabbed for it. It was older and more worn than the others and peppered with worm holes, but whole and intact. I stood there stunned. There were no other large shells anywhere about, just some small fragments of other kinds of shells. I had never before seen a whole shell of any kind on this beach.

The Whelk From Matanzas

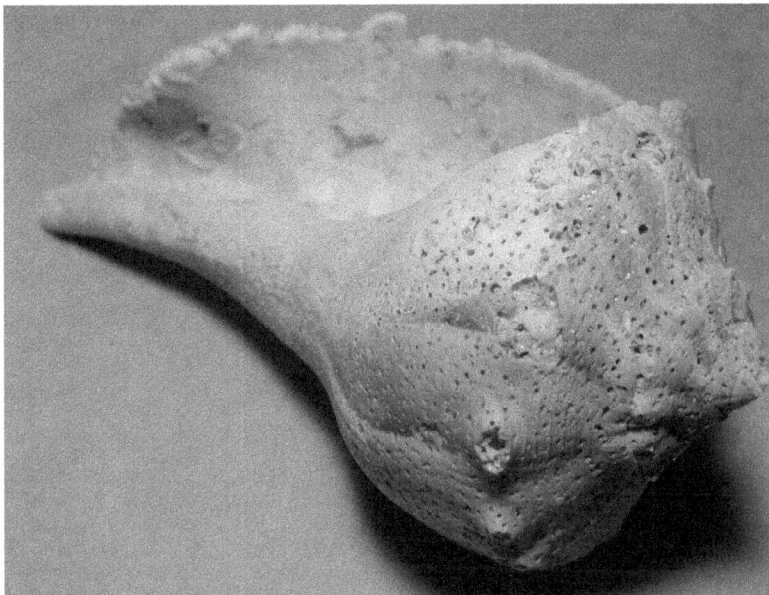

Grasping my treasure, I peered into the water where it had been. I really don't know why. I don't know what I expected to see. Then, through the foam, I spotted a splash of red. "Better be careful –don't see much red in the surf," I thought to myself. Hesitantly, I grasped at the redness.

Wow! I had received a bonus gift! Not only another whelk to show that God remembers our other times together, but something special to delight me even more: two colorful barnacle clusters.

Strolling Onward

Just know this: I was at the beach for 6 hours that day and I walked in the surf for more than an hour and a half total, and these were the only whole shells these searching eyes saw on that beach, that day or any other.

"Wouldn't it be something if . . .?" I had thought.
Indeed, It WAS "<u>something</u>."

It felt like God was saying to me, "Welcome back to our special place!" 1993, 1999, 2008.

I remember when God showed me that He not only loves me but He knows me and remembers me and is ready to give me exactly that gift that will bless me the most, even if I have not even imagined it.

It's Good

It was breakfast time again. I had been praising the Lord for the day and the food and His Word. This day I was quite willing to allow His Word to distract me from the delights of my breakfast. After all, I rather spend time with Him than with an apple turnover.

But, my mind kept drifting away from the Word I was trying to read. It simply would not pay attention! Unruly mind! It kept going back to some thoughts I had been having in recent days. They were not new to me but had just come to the forefront with new vigor, new impetus. They wanted my attention. I found I really wanted to express them more clearly than I had ever done before. I promised myself I would do something like that soon.

Then it happened. If my mind had generated a strong discourse on the topic, I would have been gratified. I would have thanked the Holy Spirit for His kind act of inspiration. But it wasn't prose that came to me. It was something not only very unusual, but strangely complete. It was a poem! With a pastry in my left hand and a pen in my right hand I began to write. I only expected a few couplets. After all, poems weren't really "my thing" at all.

The words came. The phrases multiplied, Stanzas came into being. A story was told. Then a conclusion was reached. It was over. All done. The thoughts I had been dwelling on were all neatly arrayed before me. It was good.

It's Good

Here are those words so graciously given that day.

I strolled a sunlit path today
And felt the pleasant warmth.
I saw the yellow glow of day.
My spirit sang with joy.

I watched a flower's bloom come forth.
My eye had such delight!
I felt a gentle breeze come by.
My tensions all took flight.

How can it be, that I, a man,
A small created thing,
Can joy and love these many things?
Where does this sense begin?

Why is it mine to be so blessed?
Why does my soul rejoice,
To see the growing bud unfold,
To hear the cardinals voice?

Aha. I see. God made these things.
He made these things for me!
When He was done, He looked on them,
And said, "It's good, it's good."

I Remember When . . .

He made me in His image, so,
My view is just like His.
We look and see and say as one,
"It's good, so very Good."

And every day in every way,
We're blessed by His creation.
We look and see and smile as one,
It's good, so very good.

Not only do I see with Him
These wonders of His grace,
But I am one He made to live
And fill this wondrous place.

I too am formed to please and bless,
To honor and obey.
Oh Lord, when you now look at me,
Does joy perfume your day?

Am I a blessing in your sight,
Among the birds and skies?
Does pleasure flow in your pure heart
When I am in your eyes?

My God, I will it to be so!
My greatest joy in life -
My Saviors heart to bless each day,
And hear, "It's good, it's good."

> *I remember when* God used these few moments to translate the awe locked in my heart into words on paper that I could share with others.

Reaching Out

In the year 1513 Ponce de Leon landed on the northeast coast of what is now the State of Florida. He claimed the land for Spain and named it La Florida. The exact place of his landing is still subject to study.

In the years that followed, it was the ongoing desire of the Spanish King to establish a permanent colony in the area. At last, in 1565, it became possible.

On September 4,1565, Pedro Menendez de Aviles, commander of a Spanish fleet and commissioned to act on behalf of the King of Spain, approached the uncharted coast. Shortly, Pedro Menendez found what looked like a good harbor for his fleet. He named the place San Agustin. As commander of the fleet his assigned responsibilities were two-fold: Establish a permanent settlement and preach the gospel to the Indians.

On September 6, a landing party was sent ashore. It consisted of a priest by the name of Francisco Lopez de Mendoza Grajales who was the fleet's chaplain, and two companies of infantry. They were greeted and aided by a large number of local natives. Chaplain Lopez is sometimes called the "First Pastor" of the United States. He and his helpers set to work at once to establish a place of worship in the rustic environment of this new land.

When General Menendez came ashore two days later on the 8th of September, he was met by Chaplain Lopez, bearing a cross. Menendez marched up to the cross, knelt, and kissed it, and proclaimed this land in the Name of God (Nombre de Dios.) In this way the Admiral of this small fleet, the authorized spokesman for the King of Spain, testified to all assembled, Spanish and native alike, that the Cross of Christ was worthy of honor and his mission was to bring honor to it.

From then on this place was called Nombre de Dios, Name of God. It is still called that today. The Mission Nombre de Dios has presented the cross of Christ for almost 450 years. In the early years, it established over 140 missionary outposts as far south as the Keys of Florida, as far north as Chesapeake Bay, and as far west as Pensacola. The City of Saint Augustine grew up around the Mission.

In the centuries that followed, the area changed hands many times. The Spanish, the English and at last Americans ruled the area. In the process both the City of St. Augustine and the Name of God Mission were destroyed and rebuilt several times on the same sites.

In the year 1965 the City of St. Augustine, the oldest city in the country, was about to celebrate the 400th anniversary of it's founding. To join in the celebration of their shared history, the Mission "Name of God" embarked on a major project.

A site on the Mission grounds, close to the original landing point was selected. On that site a magnificent emblem of that day of landing was erected. A Great Cross, 208 feet tall, built of shimmering stainless steel, visible far and wide in

I Remember When . . .

the Saint Augustine area, was constructed. Now, nearly 50 years later, it still stands as a beacon of testimony to the millions of visitors who annually flock to the St. Augustine area.

President John F. Kennedy visited the city in 1962. He is recorded as saying the Name of God Mission with the Great Cross is "the most sacred piece of ground in North America." I visited the Great Cross several times recently. My mission was to pray that it's message would flow out through this whole city that now surrounds it. I wanted to saturate the area with the presence of the Holy Spirit. My hope was that the visitors would carry away with themselves that personal conviction that only the Holy Spirit can fan and only the blood of Christ can subdue.

One day recently, I climbed the few steps to walk on the great brick plaza that surrounds the base of Cross. I could not bend my neck back far enough to look up and see the top of the Cross. At 208 feet tall it outreaches the greatest waterfall in North America, Niagara Falls, which is only 165 feet.

The sun shone down brightly. I walked to the eastern edge of the plaza, with my back to the cross. I stood there, looking out at the bay from which the missionaries had come so long ago. Bright green islets of waving grass and rippling blue waters filled my view. There was a breeze, and motion in the grass and water, and yet on that bright sunny day there was peace. It was beautiful - but a bit too warm to stand there very long.

Soon I realized that the afternoon sun, beating down on my head was becoming less than comfortable. I delayed my departure. It was too pretty to leave.

Finally, reluctantly, I turned to my left and began to walk to the other side of the plaza. I was walking but somehow my eyes were still focused on that beautiful scene.

Then, suddenly, unexpectedly, I was in the shade! I felt pleasant relief sweep over my sun-drenched body. I was shielded from the brightness of the noon-day sun. I craned my neck, leaned way back and looked up those 208 feet to see a bright blue sky with the glaring sun blocked out by the cross. I was standing in the shadow of the Cross!

Revelation came quickly. Yes, I am in the shadow of the cross. I live in the shadow of the cross. In the shadow of the cross is peace, safety, protection – all the things that make up love. It is the Cross, the sacrifice made there, that protects me from every assault aimed at me. As I stand in the shadow of the Cross, no harm can invade my life. My safety and security do not come from my own efforts. Without the cross they are nothing. I must remember always to position myself in the shadow of the Cross.

And so it was that one more raindrop of understanding fell upon me that day. Once more, as is so often the case, I came to minister and He ministered to me.

A few days later my attention was called to the scripture verse found at 1 Cor. 1:18

> *For the preaching of the CROSS is to them that perish foolishness; but unto us which are saved it is the power of God.*

I remember when God used the soothing shadow of a man made symbol to remind me of the infinite power, peace and provision of His presence in our lives.

I Remember When . . .

What I Think

This is a testimony, a report, about God, His grace, His love, and His ever-presence. In fact, this is three testimonies, linked together by similar events in quite different circumstances.

The first testimony is that God is always with us, listening to our hearts, rejoicing in our communion with Him. When we include Him in our lives, He participates in a wonderful way.

The second testimony is that God takes delight in bringing delight to His people, because He loves them and His desire toward them is good.

The third testimony is that God commands time, so His deeds are done in season and in the exact fullness of time, never early, never late.

What do I think? I think that I must say "Thank You" to my God who loves me so much. And, I must say about all those "God Times,"

I Remember When . . .

About The Author

The Author of each of these stories is God, who
loves us and ministers to us daily, often without our
awareness.

The recorder of each of these stories is Brother Al, a
blessed man all the days of his life, because the
Holy Spirit of God has hovered about him day by
day, whispering love and wisdom. Some times I
even heard and heeded.

Oh, what a joyful time we have had together, God
and I, remembering and recording these wonderful
times